All Right for Some!

All Right for Some!
The problem of sexism

JANE L. THOMPSON

Hutchinson
London   Melbourne   Sydney   Auckland   Johannesburg

For Jay, Jordan and Saul

Hutchinson Education

An imprint of Century Hutchinson Ltd

62–65 Chandos Place, Covent Garden,
London WC2N 4NW

Century Hutchinson Publishing Group (Australia) Pty Ltd
16–22 Church Street, Hawthorn, Melbourne, Victoria 3122

Century Hutchinson Group (NZ) Ltd
32–34 View Road, PO Box 40–086, Glenfield, Auckland 10

Century Hutchinson Group (SA) (Pty) Ltd
PO Box 337, Bergvlei 2012, South Africa

First published 1986
© Jane L. Thompson 1986

Editor: Jenny Wood
Designer: Sue Lacey
Illustrators: Ray Burrows, Graham Humphreys, Cath Jackson,
Gillies MacKinnon, Paula Youens

Set in Helvetica Light by
Words & Pictures Ltd, Thornton Heath, Surrey

Printed and bound in Great Britain

British Library Cataloguing in Publication Data

Thompson, Jane L.
  All Right for Some.
  I. Women—Social conditions
  I. Title
  305.4'2   HQ1154

ISBN 0 09 164721 5

Contents

Introduction	7
Stereotyping	9
Happy families	10
Me Tarzan, you Jane!	11
Family album	15
Equal education?	23
Equal job opportunities?	33
Equal pay for equal work?	44
Equal rights?	45
The Union makes us strong — or does it?	48
Selling sexism	51
Thanks a million!	60
Friends and lovers	63
Manpower	73
Violence against women	78
The Women's Movement	84
Useful addresses	93

Acknowledgements

The Publisher's thanks are due to the following for permission to reproduce copyright photographs:

All-Sport (UK) Ltd: page 57 (bottom right); BBC Copyright Photographs: page 56 (top and bottom right); BBC Hulton Picture Library: pages 24 (bottom left and right), 25 (top left, centre left, top right, bottom right), 26 (bottom right), 38, 39, 49 (top left); Derek Bishton: page 49 (centre left); Diane Ceresa: page 35; Anita Corbin: page 65; Format Photographers Ltd: pages 5, 12, 22, 33, 63 (top); John Gorman: page 49 (top right); Henry Grant: pages 26 (bottom left, bottom left inset, top right), 91; The Greater London Council Photograph Library: page 26 (top left); Alan Grisbrook, Camera Press London: page 56 (top left); Guildhall Library, City of London: page 24 (top); Judy Harrison: pages 36, 49 (centre right); HM Naval Base, Portsmouth: page 34; Leeds Postcards/Some Girls: page 81; London Weekend Television: page 57 (top right); Museum of London: page 25 (bottom left); Photo Co-op: pages 10, 23 (right), 26 (centre right), 48 (centre right), 49 (bottom right), 84, 86; Popperfoto: page 23 (left); Jill Posener: page 51; Kip Rano, Camera Press London: page 56 (bottom left); David Richardson: pages 11, 63 (centre and bottom), 66; Tony Stone Photolibrary – London: page 57 (left); The Tate Gallery, London: page 24 (centre); Trades Union Congress Library: pages 48 (top left, top right, centre left), 48/49; Val Wilmer: pages 48 (bottom left), 80; Yorkshire Post: page 14.

Special thanks are due to Sheba Feminist Publishers, 10A Bradbury Street, London N16 8JN for permission to reproduce all extracts from *Girls Are Powerful*, published by Sheba at £3.95.

Introduction

A word to students

We hope this book will make you think and encourage you to question some of the things that go on around you. We hope it makes you examine your own life, behaviour and feelings. It's a book about people's views of each other and the relationships between girls and boys, women and men. It looks at the ways in which the relationships between the sexes are still not nearly as fair and equal as they should be. Do you know that although women make up half the world's population and do two-thirds of the world's work, they earn only a tenth of the world's wages and own only one-hundredth of the world's wealth? Something's obviously wrong! You might think these figures don't have a lot to do with you — but they do. Equality is not just about what happens 'out there in the world': it's about what happens between individual girls and boys, between individual women and men. It's about what happens to you. If you don't like the way the world is, the book offers some ideas as to how you can begin to change it. We hope you enjoy thinking about and discussing the issues raised.

A word to teachers

A lot of attention has been paid in recent years to inequalities of social class, race and gender, and we hope that most schools and colleges are finding ways of confronting these issues in their teaching and organization. This book is intended for teenagers in schools and colleges and aims to raise questions about sexism, sexual inequality and equal opportunities. We have used the writing and comments of young people wherever possible and focussed on the kinds of issues which should be relevant to young people's experience. The emphasis is on questioning and discussion as this seems most appropriate for student-centred learning in a Humanities/Social Studies classroom. Teachers will need to organize this in ways which reflect their circumstances. An extensive list of contacts and resources is included at the back for teachers and students who want to follow up in more detail any of the issues raised.

Jane L Thompson
Southampton, Feb. 1986

Stereotyping

Look at each cartoon in turn.

(a) Which group of people does it represent?
(b) What does it tell you about them?
(c) Do you think this information is accurate or inaccurate?

What the cartoonist has done is to pick on certain qualities and types of behaviour which may be true of some individuals and suggest that these qualities are typical of the whole group. This is called **stereotyping**.

But stereotyping can be misleading. Stereotyped views are often based on ignorance, sometimes also on prejudice, and so are usually not only uncomplimentary but also inaccurate.

Happy families

So far as the media is concerned most families look like this:

They almost always look white, reasonably well off and happy.

Find a photograph of your family. How does it compare?

The chances are it's quite different. Many of us *don't* live in families that are arranged like the one in the photo but because this stereotyped image of the 'typical family' is so common we often forget family arrangements vary enormously. Britain is a multi-racial society. The numbers of single-parent families are increasing every year. Many elderly people live alone. Others live with their married children. Often young and single people share accommodation.

Official statistics tell us that:

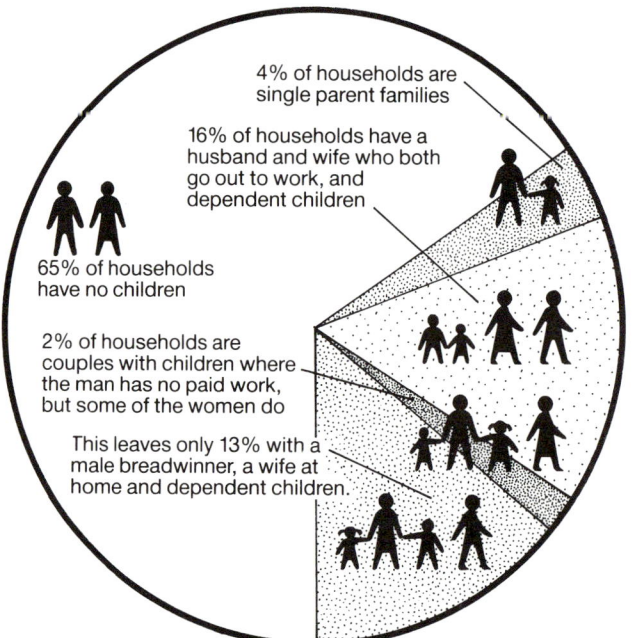

4% of households are single parent families

16% of households have a husband and wife who both go out to work, and dependent children

65% of households have no children

2% of households are couples with children where the man has no paid work, but some of the women do

This leaves only 13% with a male breadwinner, a wife at home and dependent children.

Me Tarzan, you Jane!

We also have many fixed ideas about men and women, their temperaments, their strengths and weaknesses and how they ought to behave.

1 Here is a list of personal qualities. Ask or look up the meaning of any word you don't understand.

vain strong businesslike VIRILE gentle boistrous WRECKLESS childish gossipy compassionate NERVOUS bullying AMBITIOUS PROMISCUOUS AGGRESSIVE soft-hearted

(a) Which qualities are most often associated with males and which with females? Which ones are associated equally with males and females?
(b) Compare your answers with each other. Do you agree that some qualities are 'typically male' and some are 'typically female'?

2 Think about your favourite rock bands. How many of them are all-female? None, is probably your answer. They may have women singers, but **an all-women band**??!! Well, why not? A group of young women in Leicester set up their own rock band called Perspex. Read what they have to say.

We thought, Why can't we set up our own rock band? We can play instruments, so why not? We didn't really think about it being an unusual thing for girls to do. We've been together for eight months but we are still not particularly good at songs and we lack confidence. The competition is quite something — the boys started booing and jeering things at our first gig, as soon as we walked on stage, before we'd played a note, and we were already nervous. What chance did we stand? When we first started the boys would come in while we were learning to play and snigger at us. They said we were rubbish even before we even started playing. It made us all the more determined.

Sometimes the boys say we have only got where we are because we're girls. Then we wonder if we are a crap group. But if we were, then obviously people would say rubbish, and walk out. But being girls is an advantage. There are so many boys' groups and so much competition between all of them as to who is the best boys' group — they can't do that with us, can they?   (From *Girls are Powerful*)

discuss

Why do you think there are so few all-women bands?

3 Now look at these cartoons. Do you think the views expressed are (a) accurate or inaccurate; (b) complimentary or uncomplimentary; (c) based on knowledge, or on prejudice and ignorance?

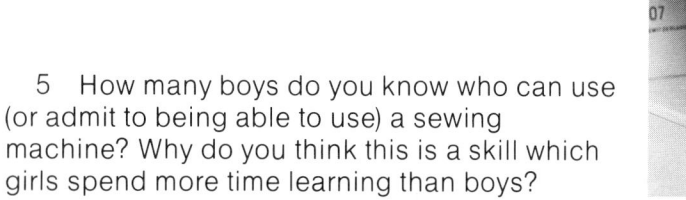

4 Draw your own cartoons to illustrate any other common sayings about men and women which you can think of. Do you think there is any truth in them?

5 How many boys do you know who can use (or admit to being able to use) a sewing machine? Why do you think this is a skill which girls spend more time learning than boys?

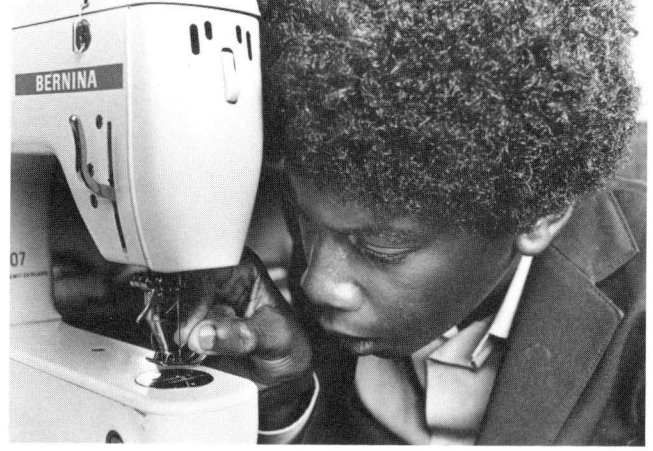

discuss

6 Here's another list of familiar attitudes about what males and females should or shouldn't do. Discuss each statement together and say how far you agree or disagree.

Snooker player Sheila Capstick knows what it's like to be on the receiving end of blatant discrimination.

Said Sheila: "I've been playing snooker for about 10 years now and it's amazing what lengths men will go to to keep women from playing snooker in their club and the sort of remarks they make."

Sheila is responsible for the start of ERICCA — the Equal Rights in Clubs Campaign for Action, and is now the Campaign's president.

It all started about four years ago when Sheila was barred from playing snooker at Wakefield City Working Men's Club.

Sheila's Snooker for Women campaign attracted national attention and as a result ERICCA was born to fight discrimination against women in working men's clubs and to fight for full membership rights which include the use of all club facilities.

8 Look back over the last four pages. Can you think of (a) four other examples of male activities which females aren't encouraged or allowed to do?; (b) any other examples of female activities which males aren't encouraged or allowed to do?

Nowadays men and women are supposed to have equal rights and opportunities in life — but do they? Some of the attitudes expressed here suggest that they do not. These attitudes are known as **sexist**.

Sexist is a fairly new word in the English language although it describes attitudes and behaviour that have been around for centuries. It means believing that one sex is inferior to the other and treating the members of that sex less well in all sorts of ways.

It's a term which could be applied equally to men or women but in practice it's usually women who are the victims of sexist attitudes and sexist treatment because men have more power in our society and are rarely treated less favourably than women.

1 Have you heard the word sexist used before? If so — in what circumstances?
2 Is it a word you would use yourself? If so — in what circumstances?
3 Do you believe that men are better than women? That women are better than men? That men and women are equal?

The rest of this book is going to look more closely at sexism. As you read through it, think about all the ways in which these stereotyped attitudes about men and women prevent people from being themselves. Ask yourselves who benefits from all of this? And who loses? See whether the ideas you have about the place of men and women in society are the same when you finish the book as they are now.

Family album

MEET THE McKENZIES

Who's who?

Nancy McKenzie – left school at 15 and went to work in a baker's shop. She married at 18 and had Mick soon after. Then came Mandy and later the twins. At present Nancy has a part-time job in a factory making window frames and is studying for A-level Economics at the local tech.

Mick – left school at 16 and now works in a record shop. He plays lead guitar in a local group and dreams about 'breaking into the big time'. He spends most of what he earns on music and making himself look good.

Reg McKenzie – got an apprenticeship when he left school and qualified as a car mechanic. He's worked for the same garage for the last 17 years and is now the senior mechanic in one of the two main repair shops. He is a committed union man and his great passion is football.

Sharon and Garry – Four-year-old twins due to start school at Easter. They get looked after by their Gran four mornings a week while Nancy goes to work, and on Friday she takes them to a local play group, while Nancy goes to college.

Mandy – is still at school with two years to go before taking her exams. She likes school most of the time – mainly because she's good at sport and plays in the school netball, hockey, tennis and athletics teams. She often gets fed-up with the way boys and girls are treated differently at school and has a reputation for being a bit 'outspoken' on the matter.

Scenes from family life...

1. What tasks is Reg encouraging Sharon and Garry to learn here?
2. What attitudes to themselves and what future behaviour might they also be picking up?
3. Give examples of ways in which little girls you know are learning to be like Mum and little boys are learning to be like Dad. How could this begin to shape their future lives?

discuss

1. Suggest reasons why the neighbours are disapproving of Nancy.
2. How common are attitudes like theirs, do you think? Could you imagine your Mum going back to college?

discuss

1 Is 'bird' a word you'd use to describe a girl? Do you think the word is insulting to girls?
2 What other words are used to describe girls in everyday slang? Are they complimentary or insulting?
3 Can you think of similar words used to describe boys?
4 The girl seems like 'a bit of property' that has been handed on from Steve to Mick. Do you think that some boys think of their girlfriends as 'belongings'? How do girls feel about this? Do you think girls think of boys in this way?

1 Is it useful for girls to do home economics and child-care courses at school?
2 If girls are encouraged to do them, should boys also be encouraged to do them?
3 Do you think it's as important for girls to learn scientific subjects as boys?

1   Can you remember the books you learned to read from? How did they present the lives of men and women, boys and girls?
2   Look at some children's readers used today. Choose four and compare the ways in which they present the lives of males and females.
3   Besides learning to read, what other information could children be picking up from these books?
4   Do the books include realistic stories and pictures about working-class children and black children?

1   When children are sick which parent is more likely to look after them?   *discuss*
2   Why is it harder and more unusual for fathers to take care of sick children than mothers?
3   What problems does this cause for women who also go out to work?

JUST LIKE A GIRL! JUST LIKE A BOY!

Sharon and Garry look pretty much alike — except that Sharon is a bit taller and Garry has fewer freckles. They were born within minutes of each other in the same hospital to the same parents. They have been brought up in the same family, in the same house, in the same town for the same four years. And yet — there are very real differences between them.

Garry plays with guns and rockets while Sharon plays with dolls and a miniature washing machine.

Sharon likes to dress up in her mother's clothes and play at being grown-up. Garry likes to dress up as Spiderman and pretend to be a 'super hero'.

Garry never goes far without a gun or a stick. Sharon never goes far without Sindy or teddy.

Sharon likes to paint quietly or make cakes. Garry likes to play rough and tumble and climb trees.

Make a study of some children you know who are about the same age as Sharon and Garry. Show your findings in the form of a chart, like this.

Questions to ask	Name of child	Name of child	Name of child	Name of child
How do they dress?				
How do they behave?				
What toys do they play with?				
What games do they like?				
Which TV programmes do they enjoy?				
Which TV characters do they copy?				

Using the information you have collected, would you say that the children have a clear idea of whether they're boys or girls?

People used to think that the differences between males and females were to do with differences in the way their bodies are made up. It's not so long ago that experts believed that women had smaller brains than men and were therefore less intelligent. They also believed that menstruation sapped women's strength.

It's now known that most of the differences between men and women in our society are not so much to do with biology as social conditioning (the way they are treated by others and the ways in which they are encouraged to fit in with what society thinks is normal and proper behaviour for males and females). From the second children are born they are labelled either boy or girl and they begin to be treated accordingly.

Once they become toddlers the process speeds up and by the time they reach primary school most children are very much aware of their sexual identity as either boys or girls.

Boys are given the kind of toys, play the kind of games and learn the kind of behaviour which is expected of males in our society. In the same way girls learn what we expect of females.

Little boys are allowed to cry, cuddle a comforter or favourite toy and play with mother's make-up or handbag. But they soon learn by teasing and scolding that these habits aren't encouraged in boys much beyond the age of 4 or 5.

Girls these days can be dressed in dungarees, climb trees and pretend to be astronauts. Tomboys aren't given such a hard time as sissies — so long as they grow out of it in the end. Once they become teenagers girls must quickly put their femininity first if they are to win social approval. It's a brave girl who continues to be a tomboy when all her friends are wearing make-up, dressing in the latest fashions, going steady and dreaming of romance.

Just one of many disagreements between **Mr Angry** and **Frisbee** your friendly feminist. There will be others! What do you think?

Who does what?

I feel really sorry for my mum. She goes to work as a school dinner lady at six in the morning, comes back two hours later, does all the housework, rushes out to do the shopping, and then prepares all our dinners. Goes back to work again, then back at half past three, and cooks all our meals. She has to work really hard.

I think the mums tend to favour the boys really. They go, 'Oh no, he's got time enough to do all the work when he goes out into the world'. My big brother he's spoilt rotten. He does nothing. He'll come in and say, 'Make us a cup of tea' and my mum will get up, make him a cup, wash all his clothes out and iron them that day if he wants to wear them. But if it's me she won't do anything. I have to do it all myself.

We've been getting little toy irons and things since we were five years old, little washing machines, dustpans and brushes. But brothers get action men. We get things that teach us to do housework, and parents give us dolls because that's supposed to be the way you bring up girls. We all do a lot of housework because it saves argument and we don't want to have to sit in an untidy, dirty house. But most of all we do it because despite everything we think it's wrong for our mothers to do it all.

Who does what in your family?

Here's a list of household jobs:

- changing nappies
- decorating
- paying the bills
- cleaning the bathroom
- cooking the tea
- DIY and household repairs
- ironing the clothes
- shopping at the supermarket
- vacuuming the carpet
- cleaning the car
- getting children ready for school
- gardening

1 Which jobs are usually thought to be women's jobs and which men's jobs? Do you think it is right that household jobs should be separated into those done by men and those done by women? Which jobs are done equally by men and women?

2 What happens when there's no man or no woman around? Who does the jobs that men and women are usually expected to do?

3 In your family to what extent are you expected to help with household chores? Is there any difference in what you're expected to do if you're a boy or a girl? Do you think the arrangement of who does what in your family is fair?

Equal education?

HIS-STORY/ HER-STORY OF EDUCATION

1 For hundreds of years, education was thought to be necessary for upper and middle-class boys only.

2 Girls from upper and middle-class families were thought to be less in need of 'mental cultivation' than their brothers. Instead, they were expected to have 'accomplishments' such as music, painting and dancing, which would allow them to find suitable husbands.

3

> 'To please, to be useful to us, to make us love and esteem them, to educate us when young, to take care of us when grown-up; to advise, to console us, to render our lives easy and agreeable. These are the duties of women at all times, and what they should be taught in their infancy.'

4 By the mid-19th century, a little more attention was being paid to the serious education of girls. Dorothea Beale, who became Principal of Cheltenham Ladies College in 1858, pioneered science teaching for girls. Here are some girls learning science in a London classroom at the turn of the century.

Rousseau, an 18th-century philosopher

5 In 1850, Frances Buss founded the North London Collegiate School, with the intention of preparing girls for serious careers.

6 Some, like Sophia Jex Blake, wanted to become doctors.

7 Others, like Christabel Pankhurst, wanted to become lawyers.

8 But although women were gradually allowed to attend university and sit examinations they were not given degrees at Oxford until 1927 and at Cambridge until 1948.

9 In the 18th and 19th centuries, working-class boys and girls received only a little education in charity schools, Sunday schools and 'Dame schools', so called because they were usually run by women.

10 In 1870 the State decided to become involved in education — first because more educated workers were needed for industry and, second, because the upper and middle classes believed that crime, unrest and drunkenness were the result of ignorance and that uneducated workers might be a danger to the peace of the country. Elementary education was made free to all in 1891.

12 Most working-class boys and girls went to Secondary Modern schools. These schools tended to assume that a girl's main role in life would be as a wife and mother. Girls learned cookery, needlework and child-care.

11 Not until 1944 was secondary education provided for all. Most middle-class boys and girls went to grammar schools, and, if they were intelligent, were encouraged to think of a career.

13 Now the majority of schools are mixed comprehensives. Girls and boys have the same opportunities to study the same subjects, taught by the same teachers.

15 Patrick Jenkin, former Minister for Social Services, 1979

'If the good Lord had intended us all having equal rights to go out to work and to behave equally, you know he really wouldn't have created man and woman.'

14 But it's not quite so simple ... girls are still much more likely to do arts, commercial and domestic subjects. Boys are much more likely to do maths, technical and scientific subjects.

'EXPERTS BELIEVE THAT...'

1. Girls and boys have equal ability at 16 but girls are more likely to leave school and boys are more likely to stay on.

2. Girls are more likely to underplay their intelligence when boys are around.

3. Girls make more stereotyped subject choices and career choices in mixed schools than in single-sex schools.

4. Boys on average receive two-thirds of teachers' attention in mixed classes. They are questioned more, encouraged more and praised more.

5. Boys are more likely to be disruptive in class than girls, therefore they get more attention from teachers in an attempt to distract and interest them.

6. Subjects like science, maths and technical studies are still considered to be 'boys' subjects' and girls are not expected to be interested in them or to do well in them.

Discuss each of these statements together in small groups. Be ready to report the views of your group to the class as a whole.

WHAT GETS ON OUR NERVES ABOUT SEXISM IN OUR SCHOOL OR COLLEGE...

All the usual things, like sitting separately in assembly, and lining up separately for lunch.

And football. We get the chance to do it at our school but it's been made really difficult.

We turned up for a practice and there was one ball for 70 girls! Obviously they never thought so many girls would turn up.

And over the years we've raised loads of money for facilities we don't benefit from.

Like the mini bus, which we reckon we pretty well paid for, but it's nearly always in use by the boys for matches and expeditions.

Sometimes if they really try, girls can get into a sailing group or something, but then, when they go in the bus with the boys, they have to sit at the back!

Then of course there's the subject options. There's all sorts of subjects we wanted to take, like woodwork and technical drawing, but we were told we'd have to give a good reason. What good reason?

The boys didn't have to give a good reason for taking so called girls' subjects.

And even if you do go down our physics labs, it's all boys.

(Text by Linda, Dawn, Jasmine, Diane, Cynthia, Lynda, from *Girls are Powerful*)

Do the things which these girls are complaining about happen in your school/college? If so, why do you think this is? Discuss any ideas you have for giving girls and boys equal opportunities.

School shock! Education system biased!

The British education system aims to give equal educational opportunities to all children regardless of their background, their race or their sex. Sociologists (those who study society and try to explain why society is like it is) have shown that the education system is often biased against working-class children and black children. Working-class and black children don't do as well as white middle-class children in the education system. You might like to stop for a minute and think about why this might be. Feminist writers and sociologists also suggest that the education system is biased against girls and does more to encourage the idea that a woman's place is at home, as a wife and mother, than to help young women achieve greater choice and more independence in their lives. Girls who are also working-class and black have the least chance of all when it comes to receiving a good education — as these young women know.

Our school has eight streams. When you come here if you're black or working-class white, or coloured, or Greek or Turkish Cypriots, you automatically get put into the lower streams. Recently a girl of fourth-year age came back again to this area from spending some time in Jamaica. The teacher said to one of us who is black, 'What stream are you in?' On hearing it was stream four, he said, 'Yes, that's the one I was thinking of for her,' and that was it. Sometimes a black person or a white working-class one might make it into a higher stream. The other children can't believe it. 'What's that thickie doing in here?' Our new headmaster says he's going to end streaming and we hear people say all the time, 'Thank goodness we're not coming into the new first form. I'd hate to be taught with all the thickies.'

We've had nothing but this sort of thing all the time — racist comments, thickies, dunces. Sexism, racism, streaming and class — it's all the same system, and it's all got to come out.

(Text by Linda, Dawn, Jasmine, Diane, Cynthia, Lynda, from *Girls are Powerful*)

1   Are these comments true or false in your experience? Give as many examples as you can to support your answer.
2   If you are in a mixed school or college, make a list of the ways in which you think boys and girls are treated differently.
3   If you are in a single-sex school or college, make a list of the ways in which you think you are being encouraged to learn stereotyped ideas about your sex.
4   In what ways are teachers and pupils in your school or college trying to overcome sexism?
5   Have a look at the 'Educational Obstacle Race' on the next page. Of course it's a generalization and not true of everyone's experience. Lots of boys aren't encouraged to stay on at school either. Lots of boys and girls don't want to! But in general, the obstacles to getting a good education are made worse if schools and school pupils have sexist attitudes about what girls should learn. Interview some women of your mother's generation. Ask them when they left school; whether they thought teachers and parents gave more importance to boys' education than girls'; and whether — if they had their chance over again — they would make the same choices as far as education is concerned.

THE EDUCATIONAL OBSTACLE RACE

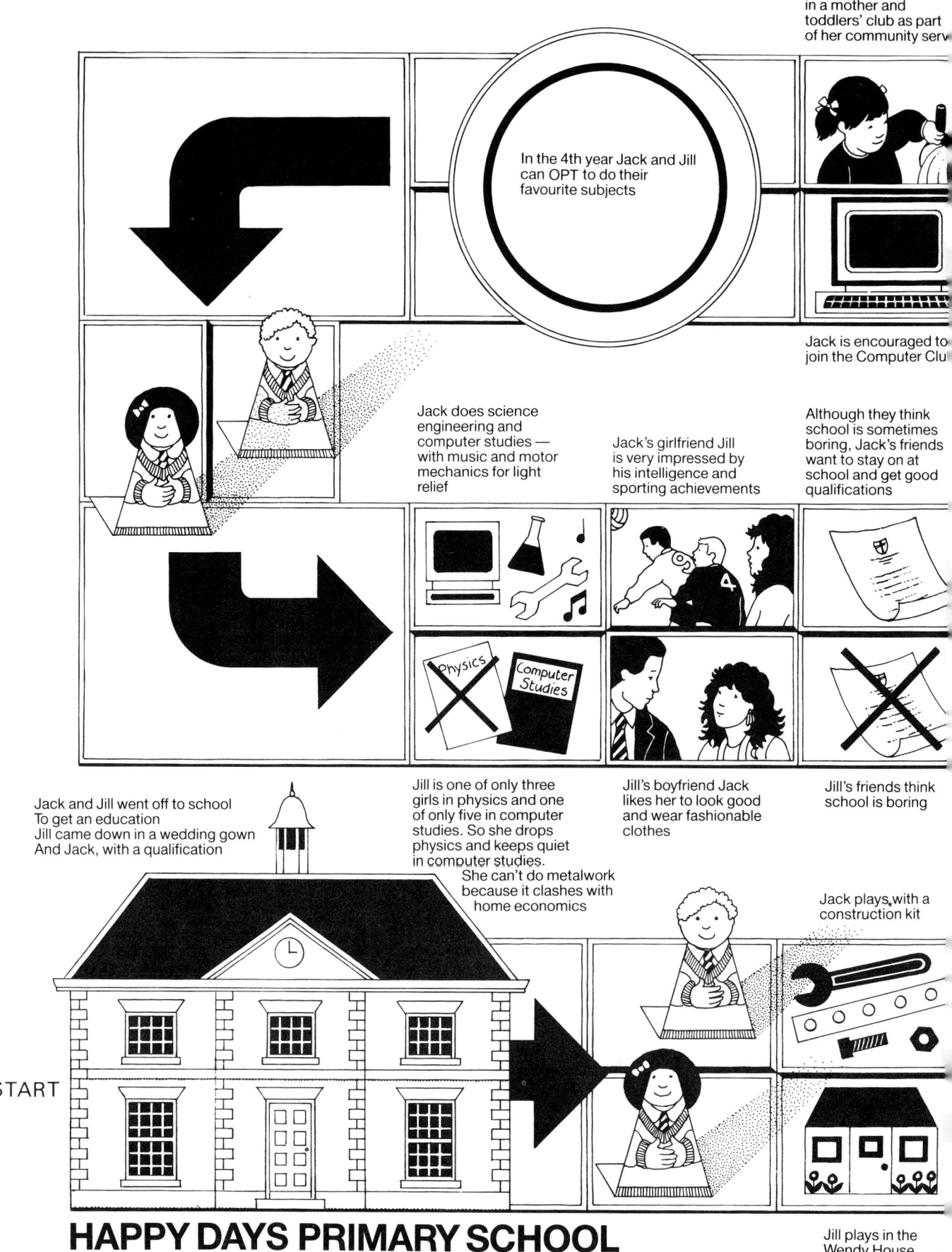

In History, they learn about the Romans, medieval castles, great explorers and the Second World War. Few women are mentioned by name

Jill learns how to iron shirts, clean a toilet and feed a large family on a small budget in home economics

Biology they learn about Descent of Man. English, Art and Music they rn about Man's cleverness

Jack learns how to make toffee apples in home economics and is let-off homework if it clashes with a school soccer match

Jack and the boys get all the attention in woodwork

Jill sits at the back with the girls in woodwork

ck of course stays to take his GCSE's

FINISH

Jack and Jill do the same lessons in the first three years but:

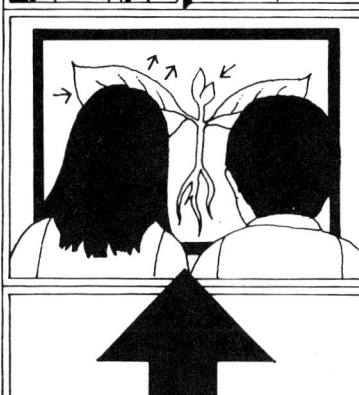

hen Jill gets pregnant e's asked to leave hool

ys football

plays Superman in the school play

HOPE HIGH SCHOOL

ers the plants and es the classroom

plays Cinderella in the school play

Equal job opportunities?

NEW OPPORTUNITIES OR OLD RESTRICTIONS?

Dianne wanted an apprenticeship in engineering. Just one firm gave her a selection test, which she passed, and invited her for interview. The interview lasted 20 minutes. The previous applicant had been a boy from her school who was given 45 minutes. He was offered an apprenticeship although he had a lower educational standard. Dianne was not.

Janice was turned down for a TOPS (Training Opportunities) course in building because she had no previous experience of the work and had never worked in male jobs before. They asked her in the interview how she'd *feel about the weather* if she was working on a building site! Bob had a Latin degree from Oxford and had taught English in a private school abroad. He had no experience of building work. He was offered a place on the course.

Girls can lose out enormously when it comes to training:

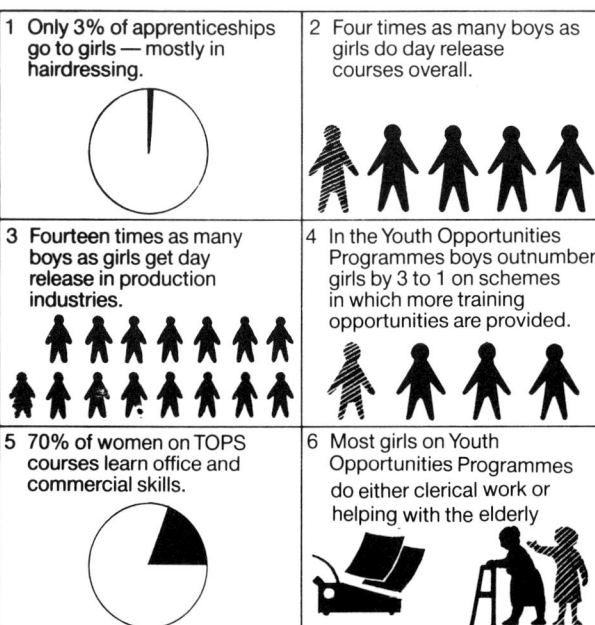

1. Only 3% of apprenticeships go to girls — mostly in hairdressing.
2. Four times as many boys as girls do day release courses overall.
3. Fourteen times as many boys as girls get day release in production industries.
4. In the Youth Opportunities Programmes boys outnumber girls by 3 to 1 on schemes in which more training opportunities are provided.
5. 70% of women on TOPS courses learn office and commercial skills.
6. Most girls on Youth Opportunities Programmes do either clerical work or helping with the elderly

Let's look at the experience of Margaret and Andrea...

MARGARET, ELECTRICAL FITTER

'Two years ago I had one O-level, in cookery. I hated school and just wanted to get out, but I didn't know what to do. It was my father who suggested this apprenticeship. He and my brothers work in the Dockyard, and they saw it advertised. The careers officer at school wasn't very helpful. She suggested a shop job or a job in a bank. When I told her about this apprenticeship she hadn't even heard that girls could apply.

'My friend applied at the same time as me, and the school tried to talk her into staying on to do more O-levels instead. I think boys get given more details about apprenticeships.

'When we started, the boys were always waiting for us to make mistakes. They thought we should be at home helping mum. The majority have changed now. As long as we do our fair share, it's OK. One problem was the way the instructors treated us. They couldn't do enough to help. They helped us more than they helped the boys, pointing out our mistakes more clearly. We don't really need the extra help. They even tried to make the boys be polite to us, stop swearing and things. It made them resent us. Really, it hasn't helped us get on good terms with the boys. There are always some boys who are quick to find out our bad points. They think their male ego is suffering because a girl is doing the same job as them.

'I came second in the Apprentice of the Year Awards (in the Portsmouth Dockyard) last year. Some boys thought it was favouritism. I got pretty upset when they said 'One of you girls had to get it'. I wouldn't like to think that I'm only getting anywhere because I am a girl.

'In the first year we had a three month probationary period learning to use hand tools, mostly filing metals. Then we had a six week basic fitting course, learning to construct and read diagrams from a small bell circuit, and a light circuit in series. In the last part of the

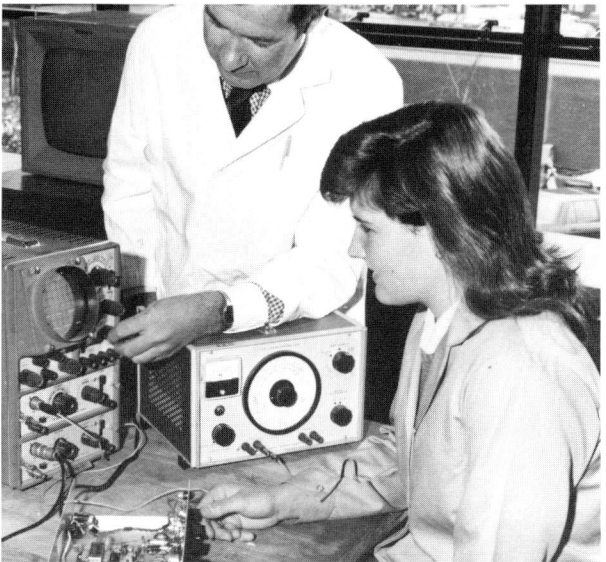

year we learned to draw, strip down and build up starters, motors and armatures [the mechanism that drives motors].

'In the second year we have been divided into groups of 25 and spend two months in five different shops. There is the machine shop, where you practise simple cutting jobs with different metals. Then shore insulation; bending and handling the conduits, the casing for electrical cables. Then electronics, where you make a radio and a speaker. Then car electronics, where you strip the electrical system of a car and rewire it. Lastly, 'pre-afloat' where you work on a model of a ship needing to be fitted, and do all the jobs which go into that. I'm working on car electronics at the moment. After this year I will be a mate to an electrical fitter in the Dockyard.'

Overall Margaret felt that though the job, like many jobs, may not always be interesting, she had made a good choice:

'I've got better opportunity, more freedom. If I wasn't here I'd be behind a counter in a shop or in a factory.'

(From *Girls are Powerful*)

1 Why wasn't the careers officer at Margaret's school very helpful, do you think? *explain*
(a) Do boys and girls get different kinds of advice from careers officers and teachers in your school or college?
(b) Is there any reason why more girls like Margaret shouldn't be encouraged to do apprenticeships?
(c) Ask the careers teacher at your school or college for his/her opinion about job opportunities for boys and girls these days.
2 The instructors seemed very helpful to Margaret and the girls. What did she feel about this?
3 What sort of skills did Margaret learn?
4 Do you think it's a good or bad idea for girls to become fitters, plumbers, bricklayers, engineers and the like?

ANDREA, HAIRDRESSER

'I liked school but I left because I couldn't stand the thought of doing any more exams after O-levels, and anyway I'd already made up my mind that I wanted a more practical skill. As I was interested in fashion I decided to do a Hairdressing and Beauty Therapy course at a nearby Technical College.

'At the beginning of the course we had a lot of theory lessons — what hair is made up from, how chemicals affect it and things like that. In the practical lessons we started off practising on a block — a wax model with hair. You can't cut the hair, just play with it! After the first month you start on real people and it's much more fun. It's a cheap way to get a hair-do but clients have to sign a form saying they won't claim compensation if anything goes wrong!

'One of the main things, though, that I don't like about the course is the way we are taught to make everyone look 'nice'. We're supposed to use hair styles and make-up to enhance a woman's "natural attributes", so that she looks more like a conventional idea of what is attractive. But to me the most important part of hairdressing is to do what the client wants. I try to spend time looking through catalogues and deciding together what would be the most interesting style to try.

'We don't get the chance to cut men's hair, which is a pity because lots of men are interested in having good hair-cuts nowadays, and I'm sure lots of men would like their nails done or have make-up put on professionally. There's only one man on the course, and when he walked in on the first day everyone assumed he was gay. When I asked why the college didn't allow men to come along as models, I was told, "We don't want that sort in here". They're very concerned not to get a "bad" name — only women are supposed to look after their bodies; and most people here think that it's unmanly for men to do the same. Everyone laughs at me when I say what I really think.

'Often people can't understand why I'm doing a Hairdressing and Beauty Therapy course if I think of myself as a feminist. Sometimes I do feel that I'm not living up to

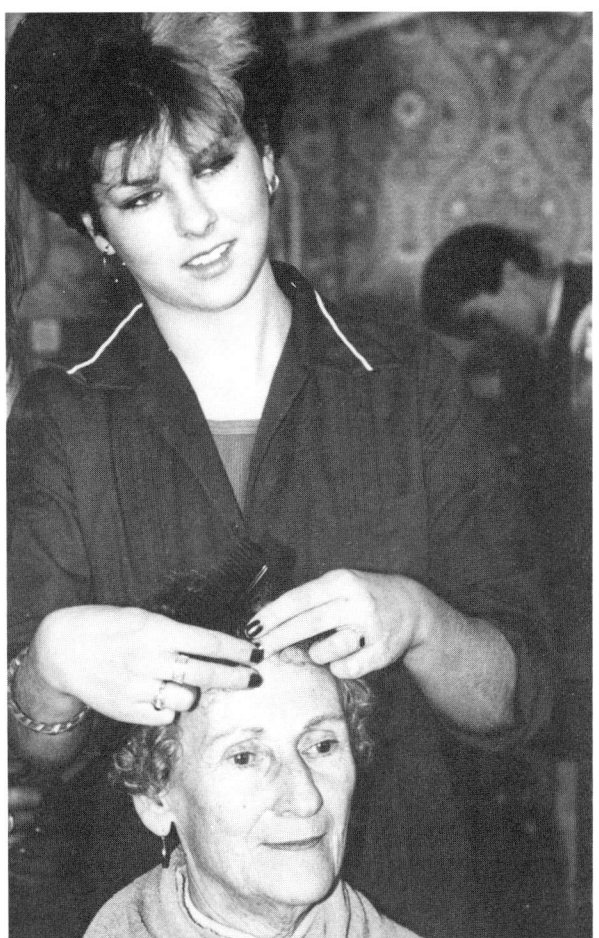

my own standards — I wish I could say that I was studying to be an engineer or something unusual like that, but mostly I try to challenge the traditional image of hairdressing. If you want to take care of your body it's not necessarily for men's benefit, you can do it for yourself. I don't wear make-up or streak my hair to attract boys, I do it because I like experimenting with different ways of looking. It's just like wearing different styles of clothes. I'm not dependent on make-up — lots of times I can't be bothered to put it on, and I couldn't care less if I look less conventionally "attractive" with green stripes on my face. My dad is always telling me that my hair doesn't look natural, but I don't want it to look natural. I want it to look bleached with black roots.'

(From *Girls are Powerful*)

1 What are Andrea's views of what hairdressing should be about? Do you agree with her?

2 Is hairdressing a good job for boys as well, do you think?

3 Why do you think it was assumed that the only man on Andrea's course was gay? What information was this assumption based on? Was it a fair or unfair conclusion, do you think?

4 Do you think that it is 'unmanly' for a man to 'look after his body'? Explain your answer.

5 How does Andrea square being a hairdresser with also being a feminist? Do you agree with her or not?

THE DOUBLE SHIFT

One shift paid at work

One shift unpaid at home

UNPAID WORK

In December 1983 the Legal and General Insurance Company reckoned that the commercial value of an average wife — who washes, cooks, cleans and looks after others — was £227 per week. But few, if any, wives are actually paid for the housework they do. Most house workers are women and all of them are expected to work for 'love'.

Make a list of the unpaid work women do at home which is usually ignored or taken for granted by other members of the family. Here are some ideas to help you.

bearing kids

looking after kids

looking after the sick, elderly, disabled

taking charge of the house — furnishing and cleaning

bed-making

clothing people — making clothes

shopping

producing food, cooking and serving meals

gardening

For women who also go out to work all of this is work on top of their other jobs.

Make a guess!

How many hours a week does the average full-time woman worker spend on housework (including child-care)?

      36 hours   25 hours   10 hours

How many hours does the average full-time male worker spend on housework?

      36 hours   25 hours   10 hours

Women do on average another 36 hours a week at home on top of what could be their 40 hours a week at work. Men on average do an extra 10 hours — and that includes cleaning the car and helping to drive the shopping back from the supermarket. Was your guess correct?

According to a recent survey in *Woman's Own*:

1 in 6 husbands has never looked after his child on his own
1 in 4 has never put the children to bed
1 in 3 has never read to them

When we talk about 'work', 'breadwinner' and 'man power' we usually think of men. But over 40% of the labour force is female and, as well as single women, the majority of mothers and married women these days are either working or looking for work outside the home.

Here are the views of some women.

I think a woman is equal to any man. I mean, I do two jobs and he only does one. When he gets in it's out with the paper and on with the tele and 'where's me tea?' When I get in I start again.

I only work four days a week. Thursday's my free day. Then I usually clean the house through and go to Tesco's. That's my free day.

I've always worked because I had to. My friend looked after my daughter when she was small. I used to get up about half past five, give her breakfast, change her nappy and then walk over 1½ miles with the push chair, put her at my friend's, catch the works bus — and then the same in the evening. I'd get home about ten to six. Then I'd get us something to eat, do the household chores and put her to bed. My daughter used to say, 'Mum why do you go to work in the night?' — because it was always dark, going in the mornings and coming back at night.

No one thinks you know anything if you are a housewife. They don't treat you as a thinking person, but as a right idiot. You don't need any qualifications for being a housewife, not like the doctor or the dentist or even a shop girl, who's got experience, after all. You're just someone who looks after kids, and anyone can do that. Well that's the idea, anyway.

Well, a woman's work is never done, is it?

It used to be amazing at the end of the week to be paid, to have money in your hand for the work you had done. It was very little money really, but to me it seemed a lot. Money in this society means quite different things, and that really surprised me. At home, in my country, money was for food or perhaps more land. But here the shops are full of things to buy, and getting money at the end of the week made me think I could buy them. I didn't know for a long time that my pay was low and I worked harder than a lot of people. What upset me then was how rude the supervisors were to me and other Asian women. Now I can see that it is all connected — bad pay, bad conditions, rudeness and lack of respect.

1   Who do you think should do household tasks?
2   Do you know of any families where the woman does *not* do most of the household tasks? If so, talk to them and find out what arrangements they have made and why.

WHERE DO WOMEN WORK?

THEN

In 1841 women were employed in at least 288 different types of work — everything from banking and spinning, to auctioneering and gutting fish. So-called progress has meant that today the range of jobs in which most women work has narrowed.

As the nineteenth century wore on, it was less acceptable for women to go out to work than it had been before. A lot of occupations became closed to them. Middle-class Victorians thought that a woman's place was in the home and working-class men and women were encouraged to think the same. But many working-class women still worked — they had to — and usually in bad conditions for low wages. In 1842 women could be found working in coal mines. This is how Betty Harris describes her work:

I have a belt around my waist, and a chain passing between my legs, and I go on my hands and feet. The pit is very wet where I work, and the water comes over our clog tops always... My clothes are wet through almost all day long... I am not as strong as I was, and cannot stand my work as well as I used to. I have drawn till I have had the skin off me; the belt and chain are worse when we are in the family way.

Not long afterwards women were prevented from working in the coal mines — not particularly because the conditions were terrible, but because many of the women, like the men, worked naked to the waist. The Victorians thought this was immoral and obscene and made it illegal for women to do the work any longer. But they did not find them other work and so some women continued to apply for mining jobs dressed as men because they could not afford to go without the wages.

Thousands of women worked as domestic servants in the houses of the rich. Going into service at the age of 14 or 15 usually meant leaving your family and friends behind and leading a very lonely existence cleaning other people's houses. Being in service often gave you a roof over your head and the cast-off clothes of your employer to wear. But most servants worked very long hours for very little pay with only a half day off a week. Before household gadgets were invented cleaning, cooking and washing were extremely heavy physical jobs. Servants had to know their place and be respectful to their betters. None of them belonged to trade unions and they could be dismissed without notice. Not only did they lose their job but also their home.

In 1888, 1400 women workers at Bryant and May match-making factory went on strike for more pay and better conditions. Working with the phosphorous in the matches gave them a disease called phossy jaw which was like cancer.

In 1905 one of the first women factory inspectors wrote about the appalling working conditions in factories for women.

> 'Work was sometimes carried on in a dressmaker's unwarmed room or ankle deep upon a slush-covered floor in a jam factory or laundry — in the same position, in the same task, every hour, every week, every year...'

In 1915 a woman writing of her work and pregnancy reported:

> 'The first part of my life I spent in a screw factory from 6 in the morning till 5 at night; and after tea I used to do my washing and cleaning. I only left 2 weeks and 3 weeks before my first children were born. After that I took in lodgers and washing, and always worked up till an hour or so before the baby was born.... I can only look back now on the terrible suffering I endured that tells a tale upon my health. I could never afford a nurse and so was a day or two after my confinements obliged to sit up and wash and dress the others.'

For all of these women and countless others there was no alternative — they had to work. Men's wages were low and rarely enough to support a large family. In 1901 there were over a million more women in the population than men. Many of them would never marry and the government had not yet introduced a system of benefits to be paid to people with low incomes. They had to earn their own living.

Middle-class women wanted to work too despite what their fathers, brothers and husbands thought about it.

When the Post Office advertised for female clerks in 1873 there were 2000 applications for eleven jobs. More and more women applied for jobs as teachers, nurses, telephonists, and shop assistants.

Others wanted the right to have highly paid professional jobs like middle-class men — to be doctors, accountants, scientists, solicitors, engineers and academics. The medical and legal professions especially made it very difficult for women to be accepted for training.

AND NOW....

Although there are few professional jobs these days that women can't do, the number of women encouraged and able to become professional workers is still fairly small.

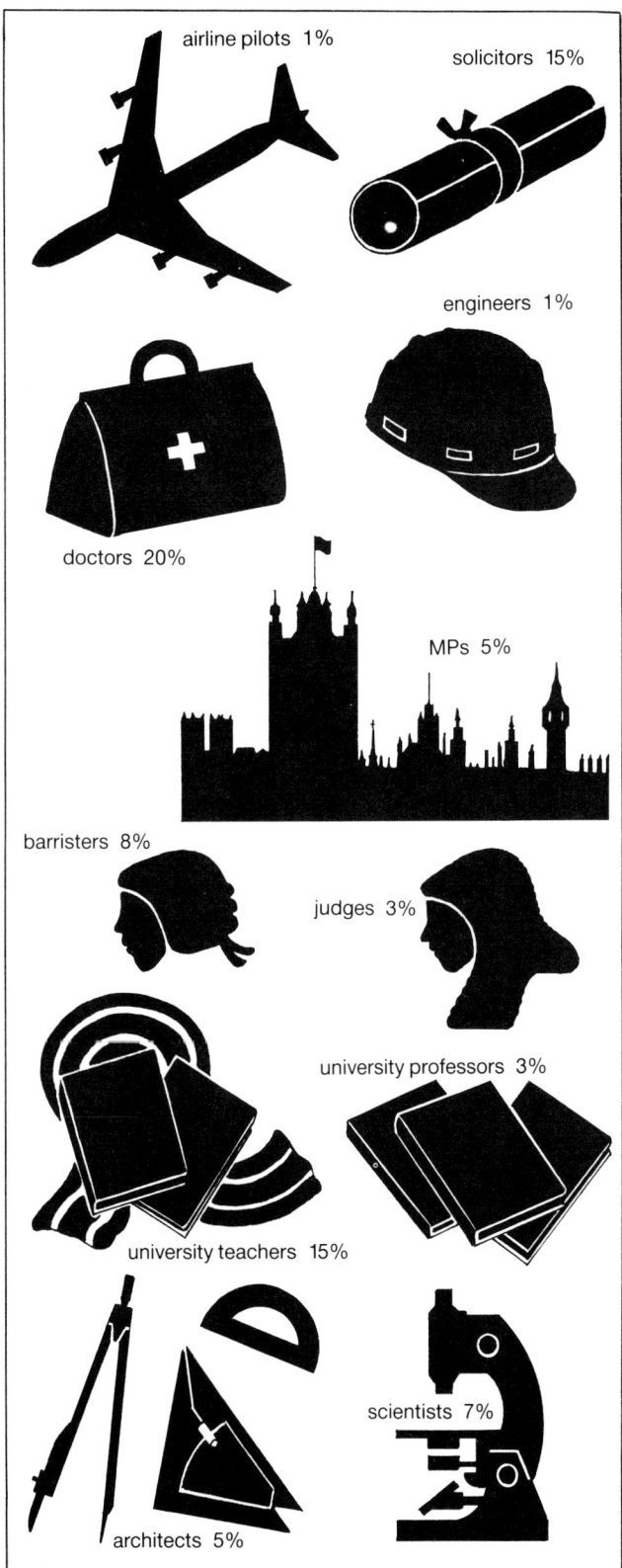

- airline pilots 1%
- solicitors 15%
- engineers 1%
- doctors 20%
- MPs 5%
- barristers 8%
- judges 3%
- university professors 3%
- university teachers 15%
- scientists 7%
- architects 5%

Today – out of all the women that work – over 75% work in one of four types of job:

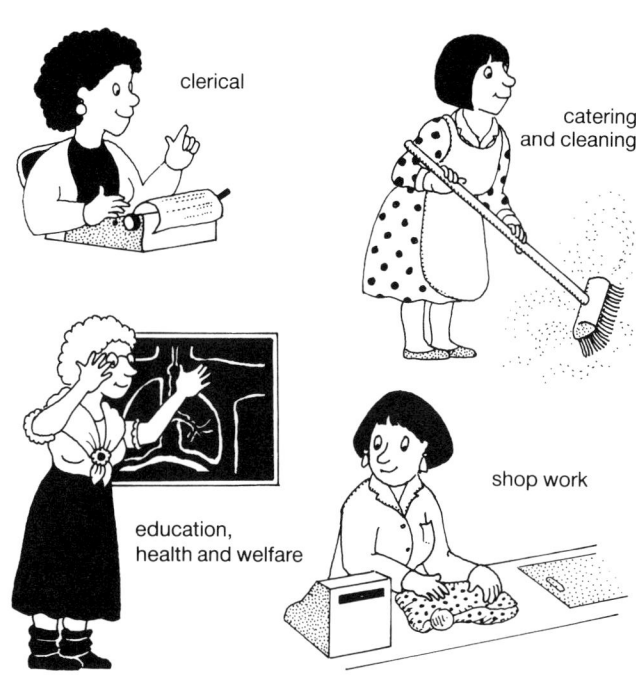

- clerical
- catering and cleaning
- education, health and welfare
- shop work

The rest work mostly in factories, and of these, over half work in just four types of industry:

- food, drink and tobacco
- electrical engineering
- textiles
- clothing and footwear

Job opportunities and working conditions are usually worst for black and Asian women because as well as prejudice against women there is also racial prejudice to cope with.

'At our factory most of the workers are Asian women. Only the supervisors and foremen are white. They insult us all the time. The conditions are terrible. Upstairs there is only one toilet for forty women. We are only allowed to go to the toilet in the tea break. If you want to go any other time they try to stop you. "Do it in your saris" they say. There is no sick pay even if you are hurt or made ill at work. And women have got ill or been hurt because conditions at work are so dangerous. One woman had to work with her hands in oil for long periods of time. She got a very painful skin rash. In Britain, workers are supposed to have basic rights — the right to safe working conditions and a decent wage. But often we Asians have to fight to get this. This is what we are doing in our factory. A lot of us have joined a union and we are fighting to get our union recognized by the firm. A union gives us strength, we don't have to put up with our employer's insults. Union organization may take time but we are ready to go on fighting. We have had a very bad time but we are going to change that.'

45% of women work in workplaces where there are no men at all. How often do you see, for example, men cleaning floors, sitting at a sewing machine or working in a playgroup?

Men have a much wider range of jobs to choose from and many of them, especially skilled and craft jobs, are rarely ever done by women. How often have you seen a woman gas fitter, electrician, docker or train driver?

Not only do men have more choice — they also earn more pay.

Most full-time women workers earn only two-thirds of men's wages. Even when they're doing the same job like teaching or nursing, for example, men usually earn more because they occupy a larger number of the senior posts.

This diagram shows the basic rates of pay for a range of jobs in a large teaching hospital in 1983. The jobs in grey are almost entirely done by women. The jobs in white are almost entirely done by men.

What does this tell you about men's and women's pay in this hospital?

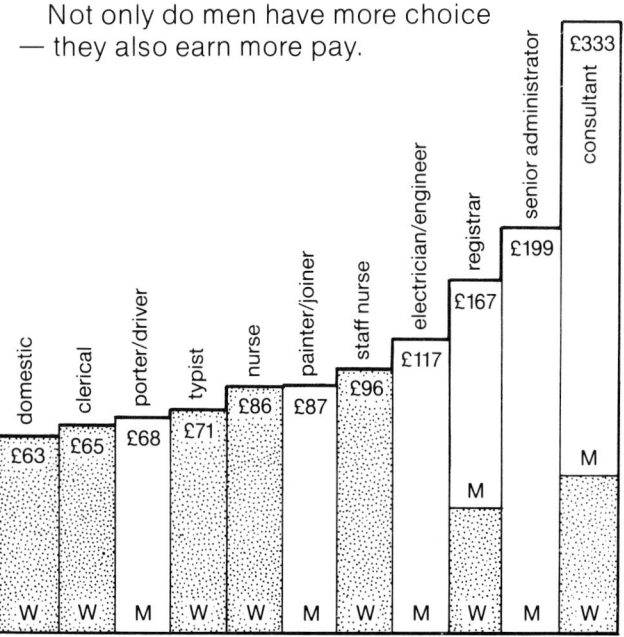

Men are also more likely than women to be found in those jobs which carry power and influence in society. For example:

Law and government

95% of MPs are men — so are most civil servants, trade union leaders and industrialists, barristers and judges. Of the 288 directors of the top 20 British companies not one is a woman.

Warfare

NATO, the armed forces, the police, and the manufacture and use of weapons is almost entirely controlled by men. About 55% of all research and development in this country is concerned with defence — giving enormous employment to many thousands of (mainly) male scientists and technologists.

Religion

It is rare for women to become priests and the Church of England refuses to ordain women (allow them to become vicars or rectors). In all the major faiths, including Christianity, men are the leaders and women are the congregation.

Learning

Teaching young children is thought to be women's work but the more influential education becomes, the more it is controlled by men.

Only 25% of primary school teachers are men but 57% of secondary school teachers are men and 85% of university lecturers are men. 97% of those who administrate the system (that is, those who work in local education authorities and in the government's education department) are male.

SUMMING UP

1. Men and women seem to do different kinds of job.
2. Most women's jobs are an extension of their domestic and caring jobs at home.
3. Black and Asian women usually experience the worst working conditions because of racial prejudice.
4. Men have more choice, earn higher wages and are likely to be in more powerful and influential jobs than women.
5. Women tend to be lower paid even when they are doing the same jobs as men.

In small groups choose three of the following occupations and make as full a list as you can of the kinds of thing you'd need to have going for you to get such a job. How would your chance of getting the job be affected if you were (a) working-class male, (b) black male, (c) female? Make a chart like the one shown, to write down the results of your discussion.

government minister; engineer; car mechanic; judge; newspaper editor; trade union leader; professional footballer; computer programmer

Occupation	List of necessary qualities	Candidate Chances of getting job		
		Working-class male	Black male	Female
1				
2				
3				

Equal pay for equal work?

In 1975 the government passed an Equal Pay Act which seemed to promise that men and women doing the same jobs would get the same pay. Working women were generally excited about the new legislation in 1975 and were hoping for large pay increases. In practice the Act has helped only a few women. Employers have found ways of getting round the law and many trade unions have been reluctant to help their women members get pay equal to men. Since men regard themselves as the breadwinners they believe they should be paid more than women — even when they're doing the same jobs. The gap between what men and women earn is wider now than it was before the Equal Pay Act was introduced.

Mick and Maureen were in the same class at school and now work together in Disco Dandy's record store. They do the same job but Mick is paid 55p an hour more than Maureen because his job title is Trainee Manager and hers is Shop Assistant.

One of the ways in which employers have got round the Equal Pay Act is to call men's and women's jobs by different names so that women can't claim they are doing exactly the same job as men.

Nancy works part-time at See Thru Windows making window frames. The full-time women workers get 30p an hour more than Nancy. Just up the road Grasping Glazers employ men to make their window frames. They earn £1.05p an hour more than the See Thru women.

The European Court has told Britain that part-time and full-time workers should get the same hourly rate for the job. But this is not yet a law in our country and the government seems reluctant to do anything about it. The men at Grasping Glazers are doing the same job as the women at See Thru Windows but they are employed by different employers. The law can't do anything to help women get equal pay unless the men they are comparing themselves with are employed by the same firm.

Equal rights?

THE RIGHT TO WORK

What 'they' say about unemployment:

Since 1975 unemployment among men has nearly trebled but for women it has gone up more than four times.

Women don't show up so much on the official figures because they are often not entitled to unemployment benefit and so they don't register as unemployed.

Which women's jobs have gone?

1 In the *manufacturing industries* — employers have laid off part-time workers first. 85% of part-time workers are women.

2 *Cuts in public spending* — on school meals, home helps, welfare and social services. Nearly all of these are jobs done by women.

3 *New technology* is affecting all kinds of jobs but office jobs have seen the greatest changes. The Equal Opportunities Commission (an organization which keeps an eye on equal opportunities between men and women) reckons that 40% of all clerical jobs will disappear because of new technology. Some unions put the figures even higher.

When I leave school I want to feel independent, earn enough money of my own, and have something interesting to do. I want to travel and see a bit before I settle down — and even then I don't want to be someone's drudge.

When I leave school I want some training, a decent job, enough money to pay my way and to save a bit. I want to be doing something interesting as well.

discuss

It's often said that women are taking men's jobs and that it's more important for a man to have a job than a woman. How would you argue with someone who held these views?

explain

What about your own future? Do you think finding work is as important for a girl as for a boy?

What happens to the women?

> I spend all day doing me mam's housework. Oh, I don't mind doing it. It's something to do. If I didn't have something to do I think I'd kill myself, I'd be that bored.

1 Do you think society is less concerned about unemployed girls than unemployed boys?
2 Are teenage girls more likely to get married and have children early if they can't find decent jobs? Do you think marriage and becoming a mother is a good or bad solution to the problems of unemployment?

> Now I'm older and the children have gone away, I don't need the money quite so badly — I keep thinking, should I give my job up to let a youngster in? If I stay at home I know I'll go screaming mad because I don't like housework anyway... but I feel guilty because there are so many youngsters out of work.

> School meals, day-care for the elderly and home-help services have all been cut in this authority as the result of government spending cuts. We have been forced to lay off many women workers. Fortunately with time on their hands they can now look after the lunch-time needs of their children and take care of their elderly neighbours and relatives more easily.

1 Should women like this feel guilty about working when there are young people and men unemployed?
2 Do you think a man with grown-up children and a wife at work would feel the same guilt?

1 How are government cuts in social and welfare services affecting women particularly?
2 Do you think it's fair that women should be expected to take care of the young, the elderly and the sick at home without payment when once women were paid proper wages to do these jobs as part of the health and welfare services?

> Nobody thinks of me as unemployed. When I had a job nobody thought it was important. I was always Jack's wife or Lucy's mother. I was a housewife and I still am.

1 Why is it easy for women's unemployment to be unrecognized and seem invisible?

The Union makes us strong

Women have a fine history of fighting for their rights at work.

1875: Women weavers in Dewsbury went on strike against pay cuts and won. This was their strike committee — which became the nucleus for a trade union.

1908: Mary MacArthur, founder of the National Federation of Women Workers, addresses a meeting in Trafalgar Square. Women played a big role in the pre-war wave of union action.

Ford sewing machinists' strike 1968: Women machinists voted to strike for an up-grading of their work and skills. Pay rates went up from 85% to 92% of men's, but the re-grading claim was still being fought in 1983.

Nursery occupation 1980: Nightingale Nursery in Wandsworth was occupied for 3 months by staff and parents. They were fighting council plans to shut it as part of spending cuts. This fight was lost — but the fight for nurseries goes on...

Right, **Lee Jeans occupation 1981:** Women at Lee Jeans in Scotland occupied their factory for 7 months to fight closure. 140 jobs were saved and a new management took over.

Left, **Abortion Rights Demo 1979:** Pressure from women has made abortion rights a trade union issue. Thousands took part in this TUC demo against the Corrie Bill.

—or does it?

1914: A factory-gate meeting during a strike of 1,000 women at Morton's, Millwall.

1936: Women played their part in the depression years in campaigns against unemployment and cuts in benefits. Here women march against a new 'means test' for unemployment benefit.

Supreme Quilting, Smethwick 1982: Asian women were on strike for 12 weeks for union recognition and better wages. Black women have been at the forefront of many union struggles for recognition.

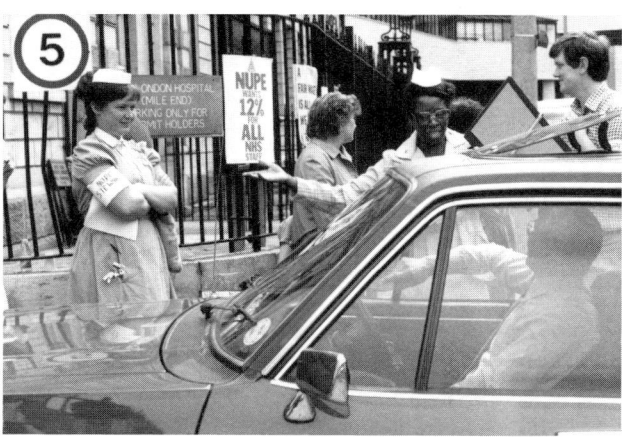

Health Workers' dispute 1982: The issue was low pay for nurses and ancillary workers — the bulk of whom are women. The bitter 8-month dispute won only minor concessions — but put the spotlight on low pay.

Picket of South London Hospital, March 1983, against possible closure.

Thousands of women like the ones pictured here have taken action in recent years on all the issues covered in this book — often supported by men. But there is still a long way to go....

Today a third of all trade union members and the majority of new recruits are women. But do trade unions really take their women members seriously?

How do these attitudes make it difficult for women to play an active part in trade union affairs?

Selling sexism

If Mick and Mandy McKenzie lived in a completely *empty* environment there'd be nothing around to influence their attitudes. It's hard to imagine what such an environment would be like!

The real world is rather different. Whatever kind of society we live in there are millions of messages around us influencing the way we dress, think, behave and feel. In societies like Britain, influencing people in this way is closely tied up with big business and making money. Commercial influences can provide entertainment and offer pleasure and fun — but they usually also encourage attitudes and behaviour which don't exactly help to achieve harmony or equality.

The real world that Mick and Mandy live in would look more like this:

1 Make a list of all the different influences promoted by big business and commercial interests which are possibly affecting Mick and Mandy's attitudes and behaviour.

2 In what ways might each of these influences reinforce or contribute to sexist attitudes and behaviour?

Make a collection of adverts from magazines and newspapers and jot down the details of popular TV advertisements.

  1 What images of (a) men (b) women and (c) children are most common in adverts?
Here are some words to help you:
   strong, tough, kind, capable, trustworthy, clever, sexy, feminine, slim, motherly.
  2 Can you find any examples of advertisements that say anything serious about the fact that
      (a) lots of people are poor?
      (b) Britain is a multi-racial society?
      (c) women are other things besides sex objects
         or housewives?
      (d) men are other things besides rugged he-men or
         helpless idiots?
  3 How influential is advertising in your opinion when it comes to encouraging sexist ideas about males and females in society?
  4 If you had the power to introduce rules to restrict sexism in advertising what rules would you introduce?

THE POP MUSIC BUSINESS

Fill in the answers to these questions by yourself and then discuss your answers together in small groups.

1. If someone were to wave a magic wand and whisk you into the pop world would you like to play an instrument or sing in a pop group?

   ☐ Yes ☐ No ☐ Don't know

   If no — why not?
   If yes — which instrument and what type of music would you play/sing?

2. Are the people in pop groups mostly

   (a) men; (b) women; (c) equal numbers of men and women?

3. Would you be as interested in pop music if there were more women's bands and more women in pop groups generally?

   ☐ Yes ☐ No ☐ Don't know

4. A lot of the words of pop songs are to do with love and romance. Do you think that teenagers are influenced by the words or not?

   ☐ Yes ☐ No ☐ Don't know

5. What about pop fans? Are there any differences in the reasons why boys and girls become pop fans in your opinion?

   ☐ Yes ☐ No ☐ Don't know

   If yes — what are they?

6. A good few pop stars are gay. Does this encourage teenagers to be more tolerant to gays in general — or only of gay pop stars?

7. Say whether you think there are equal opportunities for males and females in the pop industry to be:

   (a) pop fans   Yes/No
   (b) pop singers   Yes/No
   (c) pop musicians   Yes/No
   (d) pop technicians
       (like record producers)   Yes/No
   (e) pop group managers   Yes/No
   (f) record company managers   Yes/No
   (g) disc jockeys   Yes/No

   What do your answers tell you about the pop business?

8. Do you think the pop business is all right as it is? Or — thinking of sexism in society — are there any changes you'd like to see made? What are they?

SEXISM IN TELEVISION

Of all the different media (newspapers, magazines, records, radio, films and television), television probably has the most influence on people these days. Almost everyone has a television set and it seems that children especially spend huge amounts of time watching television programmes.

At its best television can be thought-provoking, informative, educational and entertaining. But it can also reinforce sex stereotypes and provides only limited opportunities for women to be either heard or seen in anything other than traditional roles. Here are a few examples.

Women are more likely to be newsreaders and presenters than ten years ago — but only if they're attractive. The majority of serious news, current affairs and documentary journalists are still men — whether they are attractive or not! Women, in general, do the more glamorous and 'frivolous' jobs. Men do the more important ones.

discuss Why is this?

In light entertainment programmes men appear as quiz masters and compères, women as hostesses and attendants. In choosing men for their roles, their personality rather than their age and appearance is all important. Women have to be young and attractive.

discuss Why is this?

A lot of tasteless jokes are made at women's expense.

discuss Can you think of any more examples? Why are these images of women thought to be funny? For whom are the jokes made?

Write down the names of male comedians who appear regularly on TV. Now write down the names of women comedians who appear regularly on TV. Chances are your list of male comedians will be much longer!

discuss Why do you think it is harder for women to be taken seriously as comedians?

Now think of all the adventure series, crime stories and thrillers you watch. Make a list of the main character in each series or programme, and note whether the main character is a man or a woman. It is likely you will find that female adventurers, detectives and strong independent heroines are few and far between. Make a separate list of the types of role women do play in these programmes.

discuss

What views of men and women do these types of programme encourage?

TV advertisements are very often directed at the 'typical' family (see page 10). Only 13% of British households actually live like this. Even so, it's the model we're all encouraged to copy. In the ad-man's family women are very much in their domestic place.

discuss

Why are adverts like this so common?

Sports programmes give very much more air time to men's sports than to the sports women take part in, as the notices about Saturday TV sports programmes show.

discuss

Why is this?

12 15 WORLD OF SPORT: 12 20 Wrestling from Bradford; 12 45 News and Aussie pools check; 12 50 Rock climbing — Lakeland Rock: Award winning film Climbing with Mackerel on Your Feet — sounds fishy to me — presented by Chris Bonington; 1 40, 2 10, 2 45 Racing from Newcastle; 1 55, 3 0, 4 0 Athletics — The TSB WAAA Championships from Birmingham with Zola Budd in action; 2 25 World Championship Boxing from Italy. Gene Hatcher, the US holder meets Eubaldo Sacco of Argentina for the WBA Light-Welterweight crown; 4 50 Results.
12 30 GRANDSTAND: 12 35, 1 10, 3 30 Motor Sport from Silverstone, British Grand Prix meeting; 1 0 News; Weather; 1 55, 2 30, 3 5 Racing from Ascot; 2 5, 2 40, 3 30 Volleyball, The Hitachi Cup; 4 55 Final score.

discuss

In everything from advertisements for soap powder to commentary on current political and financial concerns, the voices of authority and expertise are most often men. Why don't we see and hear from more women?

57

Start watching television closely with sexism in mind. Try checking on some of your favourite TV programmes. Here are some points to look out for.

SEXISM IN TELEVISION CHECKLIST

1. Who's the main presenter/compère/character?
2. What roles do women play in the programme?
3. What roles do men play in the programme?
4. Is the programme insulting to women in any way?
5. Who writes the programme?
6. Who produces and directs the programme?
7. How many women appear in the credits for the programme?
8. How many men appear in the credits for the programme?
9. If the programme is a cartoon which includes animals, do the animals take on stereotyped male and female characters?
10. Is the programme likely to encourage men to respect women's right to equality in society?
11. Is the programme likely to encourage women to be more independent and equal in society?

discuss

Discuss your findings together with the rest of the class.

Read all about it!

People in Britain who read newspapers every day have got ten main ones to choose from. There are also over a hundred regional and local newspapers published every day and most of them are owned by one of just four companies:

IPC (International Publishing Corporation Ltd)
News International Ltd
Beaverbrook Newspapers
The Thomson Organization

The ownership and control of newspapers is in a very few hands — wealthy hands and male hands.

Who owns the news?

Find out which individual or company owns the daily newspaper read most regularly in your house.

Who writes the news?

(a) Who is the editor of your daily newspaper?
(b) Make a list of all the reporters' names which appear regularly in your newspaper. How many are men and how many are women?
(c) Does it matter that editors and reporters are more likely to be men than women?

Who makes the news?

(a) Make a list of all the main news stories, sports reports and features in your newspaper on a particular day.
How many of them are about men?
How many of them are about women?
(b) Look carefully at all the pictures in the paper.
How many are pictures of men?
How many are pictures of women?
What kind of pictures of women are most common?
(c) Are any of the reports or pictures insulting to women or sexist in your opinion? Please give examples.
(d) If you were a visitor from outer space who knew nothing about British society, what general impression of men and women would you pick up from reading the stories in your daily newspaper? Would it be an accurate picture, do you think?
(e) If you had the power to introduce rules to stop sexism in newspapers what rules would you introduce?

Thanks a million

Teenage magazines sell literally millions of copies every week — mostly to girls. They talk about the things — fashion, pop, problems and sex — which adults don't usually discuss with teenagers. So do teenage magazines fill a useful gap? Or are they doing girls a real disservice by encouraging them to think that the world revolves around getting boyfriends, keeping them, and caring for them?

These were the lead stories featured in recent issues of *Jackie*, *Patches*, *Loving* and *Blue Jeans*.

1 Do boys read stories like these?
2 What impressions are the stories trying to make on girls?
3 Collect some girls' magazines of your own and look at them carefully. Can you find any examples at all of stories, features or advice that encourage girls to think of themselves as independent? Why do you think there is so much concentration on 'pleasing your fella'?

PLEASE HELP!

These letters appeared in recent issues of *Loving*, *Jackie*, *My Guy* and *Blue Jeans*. How would you reply to them? You can give a serious or 'send up' answer.

OWN UP

My boyfriend's very proud and he'd go mad if he found out that I'm actually two years older than him. I lied when we met and pretended to be the same age as him. The thing is, he's due to find out quite soon as I'm leaving school at the end of next term.

Katie, Glasgow.

ACCEPT HER DECISION

I am really fed up. I have been going out with my girlfriend for six months and she won't let me sleep with her. I know she isn't a virgin, because she told me so herself. I keep wondering if she just doesn't fancy me. Any advice?

Spurs supporter, Haringey.

BOY TALK
Apathy Rules

My girlfriend's really getting on my nerves. She just can't be bothered doing anything, and whenever I suggest something, she pulls a face and says she doesn't feel like it. All we do is sit around watching TV and listening to records.

How can I get her to be a bit more energetic?

Kevin, Portsmouth.

DATING DILEMMA

DEAR CATHY & CLAIRE — I'm a boy of 16 with a problem; I haven't actually been out with a girl yet.

About a year ago, I did ask a girl out but she turned me down — and made a fool of me in front of all her friends into the bargain. Now, I've found another girl I fancy, but remembering how the other girl acted, I just can't pluck up courage to ask her out. Can you help me?

FELLAS ALWAYS FANCY ME!

Please don't think I'm big-headed, but my problem is that guys always care about me too much. Even after two or three dates, they are talking about settling down and marriage. I've been seeing two guys lately and I've had this problem with both of them. How can I get them to slow down a bit? I don't want to put them off too much though, as I would hate to lose them.

HE'S MINE!

DEAR CATHY & CLAIRE — I'm 15 and my sister Mandy who's 17, is going out with Roger who is 18.

They've been going out together for three months, and I've hated every minute of it, because I fancy him, too. It's not just a crush either, because he's really friendly towards me, and I'm sure if it wasn't for Mandy he'd be going out with me.

Every time I see them together, it makes my blood boil; she just doesn't deserve someone like Roger — he's so good-looking and lovely, and she's such a flirt.

Do you think I should tell Roger what she's really like, so I have a chance with him?

I DON'T KNOW HOW TO KISS

I'm nearly fifteen and although I've been out with quite a few fellas, I don't know how to kiss properly. On some of my past dates the guys have tried to hold me and kiss me — but my reaction is always the same. I pull away from them and start making up some stupid excuse or other. Most of my mates have got guys and I'm dead scared that I'll never have one unless I can get over this problem. What should I do?

Deirdrie, Poole.

CAN I TRUST HIM!

My fella's really good-looking and he knows it. All my friends fancy him, and he eyes up every girl he sees, even when I'm with him! He says it doesn't mean anything, but I'm not so sure.

Pat, London SE15.

I DON'T WANT MUM'S ADVICE

My mum seems to have gone mad. She's actually encouraging me to go on the pill even though I haven't got — and more to the point don't even want — a boyfriend. I've tried telling her but she just goes on about being prepared. Help!

Sharon, Ilford.

HE DOESN'T GIVE ME THE EYE

I go around with a gang of about seven boys and I generally get on better with fellas than girls. One of these guys, called Dennis, is really a loner and not like the others. I fancy him like mad. He told one of the other guys that he liked me a lot but didn't know how to tell me. Should I make the first move — or should I leave it to him?

'Puzzled', Reigate.

I'M SO LONELY

I'd been going out with this guy for six months when he was still at school. Then, out of the blue he told me that he was going to join the army. I thought he was joking at first but the minute he left school he did as he promised. After I had got over the initial shock he told me that he was being posted to Northern Ireland. Now that he's gone I'm so lonely that I'm going out of my mind. What can I do — go out with someone else?

'Lonely', Hartlepool.

OLD-FASHIONED

My father's so old-fashioned that if he had his way I'd still be in short socks and in bed by eight o'clock. He always insists on knowing exactly where I am and wants me home by 10 on weekdays and 11 on the weekend. Help!

Jeanie, Rochdale.

61

BEWARE OF WOMEN'S LIB...

A recent issue of a teenage magazine featured a strong warning to girls who might start getting any 'liberated' ideas.

1. What's the message of this story, do you think?
2. Do you think Bev did the right thing?
3. Is the story harmless, good fun, or downright diabolical?

Friends and lovers

WHO'S WHO?

Maybe you've noticed — boys' and girls' bodies look very different.

The sex parts of males and females are different and of course only females can have babies. These are **biological differences**.

Despite what Mr Angry says, males and females are also fairly different in the way they dress and behave, in feelings, attitudes, hopes for the future and relationships with each other. But none of these differences has much to do with biology. They are to do with what's expected of males and females in our society. Something we call masculinity and femininity. From the second a baby is born it begins to be trained to be what we expect of a boy or a girl. Its masculinity or femininity is learned. Many of the characteristics we take for granted as being 'typically masculine' or 'typically feminine' are not natural or biological at all. They are there because that's how we've learned to be. And, of course, what society considers masculine and feminine can change over time and does vary between different societies. In Victorian times women were thought to be too physically weak to take academic examinations and no one would have believed that a man would wear make-up and jewellery like today's punks and pop stars.

Women in societies like China do all manner of jobs that would be considered masculine in Britain. In Sweden men are entitled to 6 months' paid paternity leave after their baby is born to look after it — not at all what you'd expect of men in Britain.

So although we have fairly fixed ideas about what's masculine and what's feminine — really we could change these further at any time at all if society encouraged us to!

A GIRL'S BEST FRIEND... IS A GIRL'S BEST FRIEND

❝ It's like this. If you go out with a boy once and say you'll see him again, he gives you a week. If you haven't performed by then, he throws you over. If you have, he still does but he gives your telephone number to all his friends. For weeks on end you get boys phoning up to ask for you and you haven't even heard of them.

❝ That happened to a girl down our way and she got ever so big-headed, came into school every day saying, "guess who phoned me up last night?" It was a shame, everyone knew why, they all knew what the boys were after.

❝ It's not fair, it's OK for boys. They can go about with as many girls as they like. They boast to their friends about the girls at school they've had — when it isn't true. But they'll still get girls to go out with them. It seems to make them even more popular, especially if they're good-looking.

❝ If I had to choose between a boy and my mate, I'd choose her any time. All they're interested in is if you give it to them – and when you don't they pack you in. They always pack the girl in, never the other way round.

❝ I've been out with four boys in the last six months — none for more than a week. Right now I'm going out with Pete but I don't know how long it will last. Really they're more interested in their mates anyway. I wouldn't give it to him — Pete, that is. I don't want to get pregnant and have a kid. I'd rather go about with Maggie any day. If you just go about with a boy, you lose all your friends.

❝ I'd much rather go about with Alison than with any of the boys. We have a good laugh. One weekend I go to hers for the night, the next she comes to mine. We stay up talking for hours — sometimes all night. And we see each other every day in school. She's cleverer than me, so we're in different classes but we have lunch and break together. Then at night we go to the youth club. We've been on a double-date once or twice, but it's really better just being with girls, you know.

Some young women interviewed in Birmingham

1 What do you think of the comments here? Do boys and girls *explain* have more in common with their own sex than with the opposite sex?

2 Do you agree or disagree that boys are only interested *discuss* in 'having' a girl? If you agree, why do you think this might be? Do you think this is a reasonable or unreasonable thing for a boy to expect in a relationship?

3 What would girls like boys to expect from a relationship? *discuss*

4 What do boys think girls expect from them? Do they have similar complaints to those of the girls here, or other complaints? Discuss any that are made.

5 'It's not fair, it's OK for boys!' It seems as if there's one *discuss* rule for boys, and another for girls. Do you agree or disagree?

6 What things do you like doing best with friends of your own sex?

7 What things do you like doing best with friends of the opposite sex?

SEXUAL FEELINGS

Sex is usually thought to be about how babies are made and born. When males and females have sex together, sometimes they want a baby to be conceived. But more often than not they have sex together because they like it. They feel sexy, and want to be close to each other emotionally and physically.

Sex is also about a lot of other things as well. It's about feelings and emotions and relationships. It's about how you feel about yourself and how you feel about other people.

Sexual feelings can begin when you're very young. Even little children know which parts of their body they like to touch and all children like to be hugged and kissed. Children and young teenagers can also have sexual feelings about people they're with. It can be nice to hug and kiss your friends or feel affectionate and happy being with them.

It's also important, though, not to let anyone touch you — either another child or young person or an adult — if you don't want them to. You should remember that your body is your own. No one must touch it against your will. If this ever happens to you or another child or young person you know, don't be afraid to tell an adult whom you think will be able to help you.

Older teenagers and adults often express their sexual feelings by making love. But sex is often harder to talk about when you're older. Most of the sex talk between teenagers is full of wise cracks and dirty jokes. Why should this be? How is it that for children sex feelings are 'innocent and nice' and for teenagers they're 'dirty'? And who knows what adults think! Most of them find it all too difficult to talk about — especially with their own children!

PARTNERS

When teenagers and adults choose someone to be a sex partner they may choose someone of the same sex or of the opposite sex. They may choose people of both sexes.

Most people in our society seem to choose the opposite sex when it comes to making love but lots of others choose people of the same sex. These choices are different. Neither of them is right. Neither of them is wrong. But our society is often prejudiced about all of this. Lesbians and homosexual people (women and men who love their own sex) can be made to feel bad about themselves and can be pressured into sexual relationships with the opposite sex just to be considered 'normal'. The law does not allow sex between young men under 21. Lesbian relationships aren't illegal because when the Victorians banned homosexuality they couldn't believe that women could have sexual feelings for each other.

But although lesbian relationships aren't illegal they can often be the reason for young women being taken into care.

Often, sex education classes and books for young people don't ever mention lesbianism and homosexuality — although lots of people from every walk of life do love their own sex.

Here's a list of things which people who like being with each other can do together.

1 Which things can people of the same sex do together?
2 Which things can people of the opposite sex do together?

(You can tick both columns if you like.)

	Same sex	Opposite sex
Go on holiday		
Touch each other's body		
Watch TV		
Make love		
Go to the cinema		
Live in the same house		
Go jogging		
Bring up a child		
Hug and kiss		
Go dancing		
Make a baby		
Tell each other secrets		
Sleep in the same bed		
Play in a pop group		

discuss

1 Discuss your answers together. How far do you agree and disagree?
2 What's the difference between friends and lovers in your opinion?
3 What's most important in your opinion — having a friend or having a lover?

Feeling sexy

1 What words are used to describe boys who feel sexy? Are they complimentary or not?
2 What words are used to describe girls who feel sexy? Are they complimentary or not?
3 Is it equally OK for boys and girls to feel sexy?
4 Why are words like 'queer', 'poof' and 'bender' used as terms of abuse? What do you think about this?

5 What if you don't feel sexy — is it OK to admit it?

TEENAGE SEXISM

I'm a Sexist adolescent
Boys are all I want, at present
I can hum a soppy song
Male Domination turns me on
Stereotyped into submission
By the sight and sound transmission
Lisping songs by fluffy females
Adverts showing brawny males
Teachers (men) insist on skirts
Pet the arrant little flirts
Only doing what they should
CONFORMITY is always good
Boys must hammer, girls must sew
Into MAN and WIFE they'll grow

I know every female art
How to play the proper part
Make the boys go all protective
All my wiles are SO effective
Can't be happy on my own
NO ONE wants to be alone
Scheme and plan with all my might
Catch a man to hold me tight
Forget I ever had a mind
Docile, happy, deaf and blind
Get a man and share his bed
That's what all my peer-group said
Maybe this is just a stage
Symptomatic of my age
But NO it's not a teenage game
Each generation acts the same.

Sarah Hook (from *Girls are Powerful*)

1 Is the writer being serious in this poem or is she making fun of something? *explain*
2 What is she being critical of?
3 What does she mean by saying:

> Forget I ever had a mind
> Docile, happy, deaf and blind?

4 Do you agree with what she is saying in the poem? *explain*

WHAT THE LAW SAYS ABOUT SEX AND YOUNG PEOPLE

—21 Young men can have sex with men over 21. Sexual relations between young men under 21 are illegal.
There are no laws forbidding sexual relations between women but young women can be taken into the care of the local authority if it's known that they are lesbian.

—18 You can marry *without* your parents' permission.

—16 If you're a girl you can consent to sexual intercourse.
For girls, sex under 16 is unlawful. Girls who do have sex under the age of 16 are more likely to be taken into care than boys (unless the boy commits a sexual offence).
Boys can have sex at any age, so long as it's not with a girl under 16, or another boy.
Boys and girls can marry *with* their parents' permission — but you can't have your own passport, buy drinks, drive a car, or vote!

—14 If you're a boy you can be convicted of a sexual offence (e.g., rape, or indecent assault).

PRESSURE PROBLEMS

When sexual feelings = sexual intercourse = unlawful sex young people can be easily caught between conflicting pressures. *Spare Rib* magazine asked some young women for their views and these were their comments.

> I've had pressure from boys to have sex but when I did, the only thing I was worried about was getting pregnant. I wasn't worried that someone would find out I was under age. He just kept on saying, 'Go on....' Looking back, I can see that I was under pressure although I didn't really notice at the time: it just seemed natural.
>
> Most people are very aware that the consent laws exist. Once you're sixteen you get all the cracks: 'You're legal now, you can be knocked off'. Also, a lot of girls are made to feel that it's daring... to have under-age sex; but having this arbitrary [apparently chosen for no particular reason] age you feel that you must lose your virginity by the time you are sixteen. Yes, lose 'it', as if it is something you have to look after.
>
> When you are sixteen it's true that your boyfriend expects to have sex with you. But if you do they call you a slag, and if you don't, then you're tight.
>
> I do think, though, that a lot of the sexual competition between girls as well as the moral judgments stem from boys, because they show off to each other about how many girls they've 'had'. It's acceptable for them to do that, and yet if girls do they're seen as cheap.
>
> Part of the reason I've felt powerless in the past is because sex education is so bad. It's all so biological — there's very little about contraception, abortion is all hushed up, and no one ever mentions pleasure.
>
> All the bits they miss out at school, like masturbation or homosexuality you learn from your friends in a sort of sneaky, dirty way. I've talked to my friends about everything except lesbianism, but I remember when I was younger being told to stop kissing my girl friends.
>
> Boys know virtually nothing about girls' bodies either — before the relationship I have now, after I'd had sex with boys I always felt used because I'd given them a lot of pleasure... he could always say things to me like, 'Faster', but if I'd come out and said things like that...
>
> Yes, just lowering or abolishing the age of consent won't necessarily give us more sexual freedom or control. I wish we could brainwash everyone and start all over again.

1 Do you think the 'age of consent' is a good or bad idea? *explain*

2 Do boys feel under pressure to 'lose their virginity'? If so, from whom? *discuss*

3 Do you think there is sexual competition between boys? If so, do you think it is a good or bad thing? *explain*

4 Do you think parents, schools and colleges do enough to help in the way of sex education? *discuss*

5 As girls under 16 are under the 'age of consent', it may be difficult for them to obtain contraceptives. A doctor may refuse to help. However, clinics, such as the Brook Advisory Centre, will help. *discuss*

Should contraceptives be more easily available to girls under 16?

What are the pros and cons of taking the pill, in your opinion?

6 Contraception is very often left to the girl to take care of. Do you think this is fair or unfair? Do you think that boys should share the responsibility? *discuss*

7 The last young woman says 'I wish we could brainwash everyone and start all over again.' What do you think she means? *explain*

GOING IT ALONE

'As a teenager at school, I went along with my mates in believing in true love and the romantic dream. Our world revolved around boys, and life was unthinkable without one — you'd be a failure, not quite a woman.'

'But what a problem, because in reality, you went out with Alec, who could only talk about cars, or John, who was silent, and only wanted snogging sessions.'

'If they chucked you, you felt it was because you were too spotty, fat, or boring. Or in my case, it was usually because I behaved too clever. You always had to pretend to be thicker than them if you wanted to keep them.'

'Slowly I began to realize how impossible the dream of "Mr Right" was — none of them were gods, they were just as ordinary, weak and stupid as girls were, and I wasn't prepared to pretend to be more stupid just to please them.'

'A lot of my mates seemed to see only as far ahead as their white wedding and honeymoon.'

'But I was less starry-eyed. I only had to look around to see unappealing examples of what those years could contain. In any case, my parents and relatives warned me against early marriage: "Have fun first". Well, I reasoned, why bother to give up the fun?'

'As my feeling of self-sufficiency grew, I began to see the whole idea of romantic love, and everything attached to it, as a man-made trap, to trick women into dependence, to curtail their strength as individuals, by channelling it into caring for THEM. A woman is expected to care for her partner (and children) above all else.'

'Meanwhile friends were falling in love, pathetically whimpering, 'He doesn't love me' or, 'He's wonderful'. None of it struck me as real — it was as if they were acting out parts in a play. Because women's sexuality is repressed and distorted by society, women are ashamed of their sexual feelings, and can't go to bed with a man without 'loving' him.

'When I talk to my friends they say 'But I'd be very lonely'. It's really amazing how most of us are terrified of being alone. I like it a lot, maybe because I had five sisters, so for me, privacy is valued. I like coming home after being with people all day and just shutting the door. I'm at peace with myself.'

'I can't stop thinking that most women get trapped by the myth of romance into years of unpaid work, putting themselves last. In a way, I sometimes wish I could have sunk into that safe, comforting myth, but realism kept intruding. To me, it's well worth facing the world "alone" — sometimes it may seem bleaker, but in the long run I know that I'll be more liberated as a woman, and free.'

(Words by Belinda Yates, *Spare Rib*, 1982)

1 Girls are encouraged to think of getting married very young. In what ways?

2 What are boyfriends supposed to be like, according to teenage magazines? How true is this image in your experience?

3 What do girls expect marriage to be like?

4 What do boys expect marriage to be like?

discuss

5 What do you think a woman's responsibilities in marriage are? And what do you think a man's are?

6 Belinda's friends say they'd be lonely. Do you think Belinda's going to be lonely?

7 Do you think that women who don't get married are wise or weird? *explain*

discuss

8 In your opinion, are men encouraged to hold the view that life without a woman would be unnatural? How does society react to men who are not married?

Manpower

All of these terms sound very male — how could you make changes in them to make them sound as if they mean females as well?

Throughout history words like MANkind and fellowMEN have been used to include women as well. Most books about babies and young children refer to children as 'he' whatever sex they are. The *Oxford English Dictionary* says MAN means —

1 a human being, distinguished from other animals by superior mental development, power of speech and upright posture.
2 a person of either sex — an individual.

Can you think of any other words and phrases which use male terms — but which are supposed to include women as well?

Does it matter that women's identity gets lost in words and phrases like these?

Some people think this argument is petty and that male terms are just more familiar and convenient. But why couldn't we use female terms to include men as well? Why not say 'Let's woman the phone' or 'mistress a skill'? If these sound ridiculous, can you suggest why?

THE DECISION MAKERS

In Britain think of those who make important decisions that affect all our lives. How many of them are women?

- Politicians
- Diplomats
- Top civil servants
- The military
- The senior police force
- Controllers of British industry
- Controllers of the media and the press
- Trade union leaders
- University academics
- Religious leaders
- Research scientists
- Judges
- Bankers
- Stockbrokers

How has it happened that men have achieved all this social, economic and political power and women have not?

Men are stronger.	But you don't have to be big and beefy to be a High Court judge or a government minister.
Men are cleverer.	You can't say that one sex is always and automatically more intelligent than the other. There are lots of women who are cleverer than lots of men and vice versa.
Men are the workers and women are the carers.	But women work too! And if women care maybe we should give them the power to create a caring society!

Women don't want power and influence — not like men.	Women have rarely had any power to know what it feels like. Women aren't like men and if they did have power and influence in society they probably wouldn't use it in the same way — which might not be a bad thing!
Women like to be dominated.	Many women — like South African blacks — don't have much choice. They have to make the best of it. But that's not to say they like it. Did slaves like to be kept in chains?
Women have children.	But that is not to say that they have to look after them single-handed until they become adults.
Men like power and all that goes with it — like money and influence and control over others.	People who have power don't give it up easily — why should they? How many men would give up the boardroom for the kitchen sink? The Bench for the nursery? Making the news for making the dinner?
Not all men are powerful — they get bossed around in society too.	True — but so long as their sex rules generally they can still feel superior and have someone even worse off to look down on — their wife!
Behind every great man there's a great woman.	Sure is — cooking and cleaning and looking after his children so that he can go out and become rich and famous without any distractions.

Perhaps if women had wives they could be powerful and influential too!

Why do you think men have achieved all this social, economic and political power and women have not?

Powerful people make decisions that affect us all. People with *economic power* (i.e., more wealth and property than anyone else) have lots of advantages. People with *political power* can decide how society will be run and can introduce laws to make decisions binding on everyone else. People with *legal power* interpret and enforce these laws. Sometimes they have a lot of power to impose their interpretations (i.e., their opinions), on everyone else. People with *social power* (those who are thought to be most important in society), have greater importance attached to their opinions and attitudes than people who are thought to be socially inferior. Can you give any examples of these four groups?

If these people are nearly always men — how might this affect the ways in which women are treated in our society?

Men rule OK!
Just as men have most political, legal, economic and social power in the wider society, they also have a good deal of individual power over women. When men are the main wage earners women are dependent on them for money....

1. Do you agree that men have power over women in the ways shown here?
2. Can you think of any other examples?
3. Are there any ways in which women have power to make men feel dependent or afraid?
4. What about young people of your age? Do boys have the power to make girls feel dependent or afraid? What do boys think about this? What do girls think about this?

When most boys are brought up to be tough and aggressive — how easy is it for boys to be gentle and quiet?

Violence against women

Violence against women is a serious problem in our society. The facts are startling —

73% of murders are committed by people well-known to the victim.

In 1979 the Home Office statistics revealed that in serious offences committed between husbands and wives, husbands were nearly always the aggressor.

In 81.5% of cases wives were the murder victims of husbands. In 91.5% of cases wives were the victims of wounding and serious assault by husbands.

Over 50% of rapists (at least) are known to the victims. 80% of rapes are totally or partially planned in advance.

Crimes of violence against women and girls — wife battering, rape and sexual abuse — are thought to be much more common than official statistics show because:

- Most women are too afraid or too ashamed to report the crime to the police.
- The police frequently take no action against violent men if their victim is a wife or a girlfriend, on the grounds that it's 'only a domestic argument'.
- The law is more sympathetic to the victims of burglary than victims of rape and domestic violence.

1 What is your reaction to this information?
2 Do you think we should be more concerned about the problem of male violence against women?
3 Why are men more likely to be violent than women? Can anything be done to change this, do you think?
4 Why do women often not report serious cases of assault and rape to the police?

ARE WOMEN SAFE IN YOUR NEIGHBOURHOOD?

Do you think your neighbourhood is a safe place to be in if you're female? Take a good look around and judge for yourself. See if you can get any women you know to talk with you about how they feel. Here are some suggestions to help you.

1 Draw a map (similar to the one on the opposite page) of your route home from the bus stop or the youth club. What is the area like? In what ways does it seem unsafe? Mark on your map all the hazards you can think of. Here is a list to help you:

> unlit passages; underpasses; alleyways; footpaths; wasteground; playing fields; parks; stretches of open space; street lighting; derelict houses; factories; building sites.

2 Are there any adverts and images of women around your neighbourhood which might encourage men to make sexual attacks on women?

- Are there any advertising hoardings showing women semi-naked?
- Do local newsagents sell magazines like *Penthouse* and *Playboy*? Do you think these kind of magazines should be displayed and sold in shops regularly visited by members of the public and by children?
- Are there any sex shops in your neighbourhood? Do you know what they sell? Would you support local campaigns to have these shops closed down and to ban the sale of pornography in local newsagents?
- What kinds of 'nasty' video film are available in your local video store? Do you think that films showing sex and violence against women should be so easy to hire and view at home? What attitudes towards women might these films encourage?

3 Have you ever seen any evidence of violence against women in your neighbourhood?

- Have you seen men whistling or shouting after women? Has this ever become threatening or aggressive?
- Have you seen men and women arguing? What happened? How did it make you feel?

4 Are there any organizations like refuges for battered women or Rape Crisis Centres in your neighbourhood? Contact women's centres, the Citizens' Advice Bureau or the Samaritans for information. Are there places where women can learn self-defence, judo or karate?

5 Men's behaviour, e.g., wolf whistling or shouting after women might not be intended to frighten them. Discuss ways in which you think men can help to make women feel less threatened.

WHAT CAN BE DONE?

Women's Aid

This is a feminist organization that provides temporary accommodation for battered women and their children. Women can find safety, sympathy and practical support until they decide what to do. Women's Aid is a voluntary organization with very little money. The government and local authorities are reluctant to provide funds in case they then become financially responsible for thousands of homeless women and their children. Without Women's Aid, battered women and their children would have nowhere to go and no alternative but to stay with violent men.

Rape Crisis Centres

Rape Crisis Centres also provide help for women and are organized on a voluntary basis by feminists from the Women's Movement. Women who have been raped can telephone and visit the centres where they will find understanding support, advice and practical help. The opportunity to talk about what's happened can be very important for women who have no one else to confide in. The volunteers at Rape Crisis Centres also help women to bring court cases if they want to — although taking a case of rape to court can be a terrible ordeal for the rape victim.

Reclaim the Night

This is the name given to a feminist campaign to publicize the dangers faced by women on our city streets at night. Women are much more likely to get attacked than men. Because of fear many women are reluctant to go out alone at night and their freedom of movement is restricted because of it. The aim of the campaign is to change people's attitudes so that women should no longer be seen as targets for male abuse, sexual pressure or violence.

Women who are trying to stop violence against women have organized demonstrations outside local sex shops and shops hiring out violent video films. If you disagree with pornography it's important to say so otherwise it will become even more commonplace and the risks of violence to women and children will become greater.

Self-defence and judo

Increasingly young women and women of all ages are learning judo and self-defence skills. When women feel stronger and know how to look after themselves, the streets and youth clubs and playgrounds of our cities will seem safer.

STRENGTH IN NUMBERS

It's important for girls to support each other — anyone on her own is a more likely target. Don't turn a blind eye to other girls being bullied — one day it might be you! Girls together can be stronger.

1 Suggest reasons why feminists — and not people generally — have been the ones to help battered women, rape victims and to campaign against male violence and for safety on the streets.

2 Why are the government and the local authorities reluctant to make proper provision for battered women and their children? What do you think about this?

3 What help is offered at a Rape Crisis Centre?

4 In what ways could the streets be made safer for women at night?

5 In what ways do you think girls can become more powerful?

A BETTER FUTURE

Creating the male of the species

When God created man she was only practising.

So says the old joke — the idea being not only that God is female, but also that having 'practised' on man, woman was then made better!

The aim for the future should not be to think of one sex as being better than the other. Or the same as the other. They should be equal.

Everything we have learned so far makes it clear that a lot more changes have to take place before men and women can feel themselves to be truly equal. Here are some of the changes that could help. Rearrange the list into the order you think is most likely to bring about greater equality between men and women. Do you agree with all the suggestions? Leave out any you disagree with and add others of your own.

1 Sack people in influential positions who are guilty of sexist attitudes and sexist behaviour.

2 Fix women's wages at the same level as men's.

3 Deliberately recruit women into the top jobs so that political, legal and economic power is shared between men and women on a fifty-fifty basis.

4 Introduce stricter laws to punish male violence against women.

5 Ensure that men do an equal share of household chores.

6 Change all school reading schemes, textbooks and teaching materials that show men and women in stereotyped roles.

7 Encourage men to take an equal share of child-care.

8 Censor advertisements, TV programmes, magazines and video films that encourage sexual violence against women.

9 Provide good state nurseries and crèche facilities.

10 Stop bringing up children to believe that boys have to be big and tough and girls have to do the household chores.

11 Allow greater choice in how people live and who they live with — stop presenting male breadwinner, dependent wife and two children as the NORM.

The Women's Movement

The most important voice in society speaking on behalf of equal rights for women is the voice of feminism and the Women's Liberation Movement.

- The Women's Liberation Movement is not like other political groups and political parties.

  It doesn't have a leader.
  It doesn't have headquarters.
  You don't need to fill in a form and pay a subscription to become a member.
  There are no official rules and regulations.

- The Women's Liberation Movement is made up of women who believe in a better and a fairer deal for women and who are trying to bring about changes that will make their own and other women's lives better.

- The Women's Liberation Movement is not ANTI-men. It is PRO-women. Women trying to improve education, work in trade unions, change the law, set up refuges for battered women, work in Rape Crisis Centres, campaign against pornography and for better child-care, for better job opportunities for girls and against nuclear war are all women who in different ways are part of the Women's Liberation Movement. They are women of all ages, all social class backgrounds and all races — the one thing they have in common is the belief that women should not be discriminated against in this society. Increasingly women are refusing to be put down. Lots of the extracts in this book written by young women are an indication of how much things have changed and how women are fighting back.

These are the main demands of the Women's Liberation Movement:

- Equal pay
- Free 24 hour child care
- Equal education and job opportunities
- Free contraception and abortion on demand
- Legal and financial independence for women
- An end to discrimination against lesbians and the right of all women to define their own sexuality
- Freedom from intimidation and the threat or use of violence
- An end to all laws, assumptions and institutions which support male dominance
- An end to men's aggression towards women

Discuss each of these together and make sure you know what they mean.

1 Why do you think these demands are the main demands of the Women's Liberation Movement?
2 Do any of them seem silly or unimportant?
3 Should any other demands be added to or taken off the list, do you think?

WOMEN'S LIBBER!

Not surprisingly, women with feminist ideas have to put up with a lot of abuse — from some women as well as from men.

The fact that all sorts of women, of all ages, races and social backgrounds are feminists seems to get overlooked amidst the general abuse.

1. Why do you think feminists are abused in this way?
2. Why are feminist ideas and opinions seen to be so challenging?
3. Why is ridiculing and abusing feminists quite an effective thing to do?
4. Why do feminists have to be quite brave?

GETTING IT TOGETHER
Starting a young women's group at school

Ours is a large mixed comprehensive school with quite a big sixth form. There's been a women's group here for three years. It began when three girls announced in assembly that there would be a meeting to discuss starting a women's group. Quite a few people came, and we discussed what sort of things we'd talk about and take action on. We decided to start off with a few ... meetings, closed to boys. ... We talked to each other about sexuality in general, and about lesbianism. ... And about menstruation and so on. We also began to talk about the Women's Movement, its ideas and campaigns. Some of us had known about feminism from an early age, via our mothers. A few of us were already active in political campaigns of some sort. Others were just generally interested.

One of the real problems with school groups is getting somewhere regular and comfortable to meet. As sixth formers, we are privileged. We've been given a special building ... but this effectively cuts us off from the rest of the students, and we are sure that there are many girls like us, only a bit younger, who'd like to come to meetings. We may think them too young, too noisy, but we've been trained to underestimate them. They need our support and encouragement. It's not right that they should have to wait, like we have had to, until the sixth form to have the privilege of being together. In any case, since this sixth form is largely white and middle-class, it excludes most girls from ever being in such a group.

People sometimes feel hopeless about changing things — after all, you can talk and talk about what's wrong in your school and in society, and yet you are often powerless to do anything about it. So what's the point of a group? Is it just sitting around getting depressed? Well, we think it's still important to share experiences, support each other, find out more about feminism, even if you can't get what you want in your own school. And to try and be in touch with what all girls experience in other schools — even if sexism isn't crushing you so badly in your own.

But to return to the problem of young students — they often have to have a teacher responsible for fixing a room for them to meet in, and even to stay with them. So feminist teachers have an important role here, to help younger girls get groups together and to support them within the restrictions of the school. Also feminist teachers might come up with more ways of getting younger and older girls together occasionally, if not regularly, as they have much more power than us in that respect.

Another area of common interest between us and feminist teachers is women's studies. We don't all agree as to whether it should be on the timetable as such, though we think women's issues should definitely be discussed in all sorts of lessons from a very early age — not just sex education or the occasional 'disguised' RE lesson. We'd like to see continual courses around feminist ideas, literature, campaigns, history and so on, but not necessarily just in one subject, or leading to exams, and not always just for girls.

We realize we are lucky to have this relative freedom — a fairly relaxed school, with several feminist teachers, and many special sixth form privileges. But basically we are still very restricted — everything to do with our meetings has to be checked out first and even the contents of this article had to go through the headmistress before it could be published. There's really no school with girls and women in it which doesn't need a women's group. When you find each other, it's such a relief.

Jane, Naomi, Julie, Petra, Kate, Jane, Lucy, Nicole, Rachel. (From *Girls are Powerful*)

Why not try to start a similar group at your school or college? If you need help and advice you could ask a sympathetic teacher or contact the local Women's Group (if there is one). If you want to do it yourself here are some ideas to help you.

1 Try to get a room where you won't be disturbed.
2 Make announcements and put up notices to let other girls know about your meeting. If you get really organized you could produce a newsletter or magazine of your own.
3 Make sure everyone feels welcome at the meeting — and everyone gets space to talk.
4 A good way to start is by talking about your own experiences and feelings, and about what sexism feels like to you.
5 If you find you want to know more about the Women's Movement draw up a list of topics to discuss. Maybe you could invite women with special knowledge and experience (e.g., about domestic violence, the media or pornography) to come and talk to you.
6 Maybe there are things in your school or college you think are sexist. Changing them might be hard but you could at least begin to get the issues talked about.
7 Be prepared for ridicule and abuse but don't let it frighten you or put you off. Girls with ideas of their own can be seen as quite a challenge — which you are — so be sure to support each other when the going gets tough. You'll find more allies than you think!

GIRLS' NIGHT AT THE YOUTH CLUB

Girls' nights started up here last September, and some of us have been coming since the very first night — it's every Friday. Before then we used to come to the club on Tuesdays, when it was mixed, boys and girls. It was chaos, pure chaos. The boys rush around all over the place. They jump over the counter into the kitchen. When you tell them to stop, they say, no, you don't own the club. They push and hit you. They think they own the gym — kicking footballs around all night, you just can't go in there, unless you want to play too, and then they call you a tomboy.

Just after the girls' nights started, the youth leaders organized a girls' camp. We really got to know each other, and made new friends. We all go to different schools, so this camp was a good time for us to mix with new people.

There's a notice up about girls' night, and some of us who joined later, saw it and asked the youth leader, and decided to try it. You can learn lots of things that you want to know — tape recording, filming, swimming, drama, and there'll be brick-laying when the weather gets better, and skills like that. Every week you have a particular activity — we've done ice-skating too. But also you can talk to each other in peace — and run around freely. When the boys are here you have to keep dodging. There's much fewer rules on girls' nights.

But the main thing is getting to know other girls, and getting more friendly. You can be peaceful here and take your time. On mixed nights, you have to talk quickly, you can't relax — if you offer each other sweets or chips, everyone grabs. It makes everyone, girls and boys, much more noisy, and the girls are sometimes not nice to each other — they seem more snobby, not wanting to know you. The same girls, when they come here, turn out to become your friends. It's important to have friends outside school because often your friends don't live near you and anyway in mixed schools it's the same problem, you can't get quiet times together, and it's do this, do that all the time.

We like having the chance to do sports without boys around. They are too pushy. Sometimes we enjoy playing with them, but we need to play on our own too.

Some of our friends say, isn't it boring when there's no boys? We say, no, it's better without, but anyway there's Tuesday nights if you want to get to know boys. Then some say, well are there any dishy ones there? That's all they ever think about, but it's strange, because, when you think about it, girls mainly like going around with other girls.

At school, boys are always using swearing words. Half of them don't know what they mean, it's just acting tough. Like all these skinhead haircuts, and wearing all these posh things that are in the fashion now... but at this Friday club you don't have to bother about any of that, it's relaxed, it's exciting, and every time you come you learn more things.

Some people say to us that it's not healthy, not natural to be separated from boys, especially those of us who go to all girls' schools. But it doesn't matter to us, we know that we get more chances to do things when there's no boys around. We could go to the mixed nights — some of us do, but Fridays are special and we're going to go on coming.

Hayley, Tracey, Julie, Jenny, Deborah, Alison, Ann, Penny, Juliette
(From *Girls are Powerful*)

If you think that this sounds like fun try the girls' night at your local youth club. If there isn't one, see what you can do about getting one started.

If you need some help try asking a sympathetic youth leader or contact the local women's group. Here are some ideas to think about —

1 You need the youth club space all to yourselves for the night.
2 Work out the sort of things you'd like to do — try things you don't usually get the chance to do with boys around.
3 Make sure there's a quiet space just to talk.
4 Make sure you have a woman youth worker who's keen on the idea too — male youth workers should take the evening off on girls' night!

WHAT ABOUT THE BOYS?

If you also feel strongly about changing sexism in society, there are things you can do.

1 Do your share at home and don't let your mother and sisters wait on you hand and foot.

2 Don't let other boys pressurize you into being a bully and a tough guy. Try to walk away from trouble that's going to lead to a fight.

3 Treat girls with thoughtfulness and respect — don't make dirty jokes at their expense.

4 If you see girls getting put down by boys, challenge the boys about it and don't get drawn into doing the same yourself.

5 If you spot examples of sexism in your school or college — in what teachers say or in the way girls are treated — speak out about it to let them know you don't approve of girls being put down or discriminated against.

6 Not all girls have feminist ideas about themselves — many of them have been brainwashed into thinking boys are all that matters in life. Well, you aren't, so don't take advantage of the situation — much better to have friendships that are based on genuine equality.

7 Boys can't be part of the Women's Movement, but there's nothing to stop you doing all you can to support their aims. You can give girls space to be themselves and you can try to prevent other boys from interfering.

If you've been reading this book right through it probably means you've got a fairly enlightened teacher. Lots of teachers and lots of schools just wouldn't want to talk about these things with you. And there aren't many other books like this one around!

Read through the section, 'Me Tarzan, you Jane' (pages 11–14), again and see whether your ideas about the place of men and women in society have changed in any way. Jot down your reactions to what you've learned by reading this book.

1. Before I read this book I thought ....
2. The thing that has been most interesting in this book is ....
3. My views about men in society now are ....
4. My views about women in society now are ....
5. My feelings about equality between men and women are ....
6. I think this book should/should not be used in schools and colleges because ....

Useful addresses

Abortion

Brook Advisory Centres – (especially for young people) 153a East St, London SE17 (01-708-1234)
National Abortion Campaign – 75 Kingsway, London WC2 (01-278-0135)
Northern Ireland Abortion Campaign – c/o Women's Centre, 16/18 Donegall St, Belfast 1 (0232-243363)
Pregnancy Advisory Service – 11/13 Charlotte St, London W1 (01-637-8962)
Release (advice on getting abortions) – 1 Elgin Ave, London W9 (01-289-1123)
Scottish Abortion Campaign – c/o Carol Thomson, 239 Kenmure St, Glasgow G41 (041-423-2952)
Ulster Pregnancy Advisory Association – 719a Lisburn Rd, Belfast BT9 7GU (0232-667345)

Battered women

Black Women's Group (for information on refuges for women of many nationalities) – c/o Women's Aid Federation (address below)
Lambeth Asian Women's Asha – Cooperative Refuge, Young Women's Hostel, c/o 378 Coldharbour Lane, London SW9 (01-274-8854)
Leeds Asian Women's Refuge – c/o Black Women's Group, Women's Aid Federation (address below)
Manchester Asian Women's Aid – PO Box 107, Oldham OL8 1DA
Northern Ireland Women's Aid Federation – 143a University St, Belfast BT7 1HP (0232-249041/249358)
Scottish Women's Aid – 11 St Colme St, Edinburgh EH3 6AA (031-225-3321)
Welsh Women's Aid – Incentive House, Adam St, Cardiff (0222-462291)
Women's Aid Federation (England) – 52/54 Featherstone St, London EC1 (01-251-6429)

Black women

Abasindi Cooperative – Moss Side People's Centre, St Mary's St, Manchester (061-226-6837)
Asian Female Umbrella Organization – c/o ICC, Mansfield Rd, Nottingham
Asian Women's Resource Centre – 134 Minet Ave, London NW10 (01-961-6549)
Brixton Black Women's Centre and Newsletter – 41a Stockwell Green, London SW9 9HZ (01-274-9220/7696)
Commonwealth Institute – Kensington High St, London W8
Leicester Black Women's Group – c/o 30 Westleigh Rd, Leicester LE3 0HH (0533-55201)
Liverpool Black Women's Group – Old Coach House, Back Sandon St, off Falkener Square, Liverpool 8 (051-708-9698)
Nottingham Black Women's Group – c/o Ukaidi Centre, Nottingham (0602-583-173)
Sheffield Black Women's Group – 39 Crescent Rd, Nether Edge, Sheffield 7
West Indian Women's Organization – 71 Pound Lane, London NW10 (01-451-4827)
Wolverhampton Black Women's Co-op Centre – c/o Wolverhampton CCR, 2 Clarence St, Wolverhampton WV1 4HZ (0902-773391)

Bookselling

Silver Moon Feminist Bookshop – 68 Charing Cross Rd, London WC2 (01-836-7906)
Sisterwrite Women's Bookshop – 190 Upper St, London N1 (01-226-9782)
Woman Zone – 119 Buccleuch St, Edinburgh (031-667-0011)
The Women's Press Bookclub (Mail Order only) – 34 Great Sutton St, London EC1V 0DX (01-253-0009)

Childcare

National Childcare Campaign – 75 Kingsway, London WC2 (01-405-5617/8)
Pre-School Playgroups Association – Alford House, Aveline St, London SE11

Children

Child Poverty Action Group – Macklin St, Drury Lane, London WC2 (01-242-9149)
CISSY (Campaign to Impede Sex Stereotyping in the Young) – 177 Gleneldon Rd, London SW16 (01-677-2411)
The Children's Legal Centre – 20 Compton Terrace, London N1 (01-359-6251)

Claimants

Citizens' Rights Office of the Child Poverty Action Group – 01-405-5942
Federation of Claimants' Unions – 296 Bethnal Green Rd, London E2 (01-739-4173)

Contraception

Family Planning Information Service – 27–35 Mortimer St, London W1 (01-636-7866)
Family Planning Information Service – (Northern Ireland) – 113 University St, Belfast BT7 1HP (0232-225488)
Family Planning Information Service – (Scotland) 4 Clifton St, Glasgow 3 (041-333-9696)
Family Planning Information Service – (Wales) 6 Windsor Place, Cardiff (0222-42766)

Eating issues

Anorexia and Bulemia Nervosa Association – c/o Group Links, 25 Bertram St, London N19 5DQ
Anorexic Aid – c/o Alison Cork, The Priory Centre, 11 Priory Rd, High Wycombe, Bucks
Overeaters Anonymous (mixed group) – 01-589-3157

Education

National Union of Students – 461 Holloway Rd, London N7 (01-272-8900)
Women in Education Group (Anti-sexist education) – ILEA Drama and Tape Centre, Princeton St, London WC1 (01-242-6087)
Women in the NUT – c/o 83 Banbury House, Banbury Rd, London E9 (01-533-2977)
Working Class Women's Education and Action Group – 5 Churchfields Ave, Cork, Ireland (Cork 507969)

Equal opportunities/Law/Women's rights

Equal Opportunities Commission for Northern Ireland – Chamber of Commerce House, 22 Great Victoria St, Belfast BT2 2BA (0232-242-752)
Equal Opportunities Commission (UK) – Overseas House, Quay St, Manchester 3 (061-833-9244)
Law Centres Federation – 18/19 Warren St, London W1P 5DB (01-387-8570)
National Association of Citizens' Advice Bureaux – 115/123 Pentonville Rd, London N1 9LE (01-833-2181)
National Council for Civil Liberties (Women's Rights Unit) – 21 Tabard St, London SE1 (01-403-3888)
Release (Legal advice on drugs and the law and abortion) – 1 Elgin Ave, London W9 (01-289-1123)
Rights of Women – 52/54 Featherstone St, London EC1 (01-251-6577)
Scottish Council for Civil Liberties – 146 Holland St, Glasgow G2 4NG (041-332-5960)

Film/video/photography

COW (Cinema of Women) – 27 Clerkenwell Close, London EC1 (01-251-4978)
Format Women's Photography Agency – 25 Horsell Rd, London N1 (01-609-3439)
Leeds Animation Workshop – c/o Box LAW, 59 Cookridge St, Leeds 2 (0532-484997)
Sheffield Film Co-op – Albreda House, Lydgate Lane, Sheffield 10 (0742-668857)
Women's Film, Video and TV Network – 79 Wardour St, London W1 (01-434-2076)

Health

Health Education Council – 78 New Oxford St, London WC1 (01-637-1881)
Women's Health Group for Ethnic Minorities – c/o Aliyay Osman, 8 Loveday Rd, London W13
Women's Health Information Centre – 52/54 Featherstone St, London EC1 (01-251-6598/0)
Women's Therapy Centre – 6 Manor Gardens, London N17 (01-263-6200)

History

Feminist Archive – c/o University of Bath, Claverton Down, Bath BA2 7AY
London Feminist History Group – c/o Feminist Library, Hungerford House, Victoria Embankment, London WC2

Holiday Centres (for women and children)

Horton-in-Ribbledale – Old Vicarage, Horton-in-Ribbledale, Settle, N. Yorkshire (072-96207)
Oaklands – Glastonbury-on-Wye, nr. Hereford, Powys, Wales (049-74275)

Housing

Homeless Action (for single homeless women) – 52/54 Featherstone St, London EC1Y 8RT (01-251-6783)
Housing Advisory Switchboard – 01-434-2522
Missing Link (hostel for young women who are homeless) – 39 Jamaica St, Stokes Croft, Bristol 2 (0272-428368/9)
Shelter (National Campaign for the Homeless) – 157 Waterloo Rd, London SE1 (01-633-9377)

Lesbians

Carafriend Derry – 0504-263120
Cardiff – 0222-374051
Che (Campaign for Homosexual Equality) – 274 Upper St, London N1 (01-359-3973)
Edinburgh Friend Women's Line – 031-556-409
Gay Legal Advice – BM Glad, London WC1N 3XX (01-821-7672)
London Lesbian Line – BM Box 1514, London WC1 3XX (01-251-6911)

Libraries

EOC Information Centre – EOC Overseas House, Quay St, Manchester 3 (061-833-9244)
Fawcett Library – City of London Polytechnic, Old Castle St, London E1 (01-283-1030 Ext 570)
Feminist Library – 1st Floor, Hungerford House, Victoria Embankment, London WC2 (01-930-0715)

Life on earth

Friends of the Earth – 377 City Rd, London EC1 (01-837-0731)
Greenpeace – 6 Endsleigh St, London WC1
Women For Life on Earth – 2 Bramhill Gardens, London NW5 1JH (01-272-3449)

Media

Women's Media Action Campaign – c/o A Woman's Place, Hungerford House, Victoria Embankment, London WC2

Music

Women's Revolutions Per Minute (women's record distributor) – 62 Woodstock Rd, Birmingham 13 9BN (021-449-7041)

Nuclear threat

Campaign for Nuclear Disarmament – 11 Goodwin St, London N4 (01-263-0977)
Greenham Common Women's Peace Movement – USAF Greenham Common, Newbury, Berkshire (01-833-2831/2)
Scottish CND – 420 Sauchiehall St, Glasgow G2 3JD (041-331-2878)
Women's Peace Alliance – Box 240, Peace News, 8 Elm Ave, Nottingham

Parents

Gingerbread – 35 Wellington St, London WC2 (01-240-0953/4)
Lesbian Mothers Advice Worker – c/o Rights of Women, 42/45 Featherstone Rd, London EC1
One Parent Families – 255 Kentish Town Rd, London NW5 (01-267-1361)
Scottish Council for Single Parents – c/o J Macqueen, 13 Gayfields Square, Edinburgh EH2 3NX (031-556-3899)

Publishing

Onlywomen Press – 38 Mount Pleasant, London WC1 (01-837-0596)
Pandora Press – 14 Leicester Square, London (01-437-9011)
Sheba Feminist Publishers – 10A Bradbury St, London N16 8JN (01-254-1590)
Strawmullion – 43 Candlemaker Row, Edinburgh EH1 2QB
Virago Press – 41 William IVth St, London WC2 (01-379-6977)
The Women's Press – 34 Great Sutton St, London EC1V 0DX (01-251-3007)

Radio

Women's Airwaves – c/o Local Radio Workshop, 12 Praed Mews, London W6 (01-402-7651)

Rape (Rape Crisis Centres)

England

Birmingham – PO Box 558, Birmingham B3 2HL (office hours 021-233-2122) (24hr line 021-233-2655)
Brighton – Tues 6–9pm, Fri 9–3pm, Sat 10am–1pm (0272-6997556)
Bristol (also contact for the Incest Survivors Group) – 39 Jamaica St, Stokes Croft, Bristol 2, Avon 10.30–2.30 Mon–Fri 24hr answering service (0272-428331)
Cambridge – Box R, 12 Mill Rd, Cambridge Mon 7–9pm Wed 6–12pm Sat 11am–5pm (0223-358314)
Cleveland – PO Box 31, Middlesborough, Cleveland Mon–Thu 10–3pm Thu 7.30–9.30 (0642-225787)
Coventry – PO Box 176 Coventry, W. Midlands Mon 7–10pm, weekdays 11am–3pm (0203-77229)
Derby – Thu 7.30–9.30pm (0332-372545)
Leeds – PO Box 27, Leeds LS2 7EG 12–4pm daily 7pm–10pm weekdays (0532-440058)
Liverpool – Mon 7–9pm, Thu 2–5pm, Sat 2–5pm (051-734-4369)
London – PO Box 69, London WC1X 9NJ (office no. 01-278-3965) (01-837-1600 24hr)
Manchester – PO Box 336, Manchester M60 2BS Tue and Fri 2–5pm, Wed, Thu, Sun 6–9pm (061-228-3602)
Norwich – PO Box 47, Norwich Mon 6–8pm, Thu 8–10pm, Fri 10–2pm (24hr answerphone) (0603-667687)
Nottingham – c/o 37a Mansfield Rd, Nottingham Mon–Fri 11am–5pm answerphone at other times (0602-410440)
Peterborough – Tue 7.30–10pm, Sat 10–12 noon (0733-40515)
Reading – Box 9, 17 Chatham St, Reading, Berks Sun 7.30–10.30pm (0374-55577)
Sheffield – PO Box 34, Sheffield, S Yorks Mon–Fri 10–5pm, Sat 12–3, also Mon, Tue, Thu eves (0742-755255)
Tyneside – PO Box 13, Newcastle 3 Mon–Fri 10am–5pm, Sat & Sun 6.30–10pm (0632-329858)

Ireland

Belfast – PO Box 46, Belfast BT2 7AR Mon–Fri 1–6pm, Tues and Fri 7.30–10pm (0232-249696)
Cork – PO Box 42, Brian Boro St, Cork open Mon 9.30–12am, Wed 7.30–10pm, Fri 9.30–12am, Sun 2.30–4pm (Cork 968-068)
Dublin – 2 Lower Pembroke St, Dublin 2 7 days a week 24hr service (Dublin 601470)

Scotland

Aberdeen – PO Box 123, Aberdeen Mon 6–8pm, Thu 7–9pm (0224-575560)
Central Scotland – PO Box 4, Falkirk Mon and Thu 7–9pm (0324-38433)
Edinburgh – PO Box 120, Edinburgh EH1 3ND Mon–Fri 6–10pm, Sat 2–10pm (031-556-9437)
Strathclyde – Mon, Wed, Fri, 7–10pm 041-221-8448

Wales

South Wales – Box 17, 108 Salisbury Rd, Cardiff Mon and Thu 7–10pm, Wed 11am–2pm (0222-373181)

Women Against Rape – Bristol c/o Caroline Barker, 23 Fairlawn Rd, Bristol (0272-556554) or 71 Tonbridge St, London WC1 (access) or 21 New George St, Elton, Lancs
Taboo (Manchester support group for incest survivors) – PO Box 38, Manchester M60 1HG (office 061-236-1323) (phone line 061-236-1712)
Incest Survivors Campaign (Campaign and self-help therapy) – c/o AWP, Hungerford House, Victoria Embankment, London WC2 (01-737-1354)

Self defence

Women's Self Defence Network – PO Box 20, The Centre, Oxford

Technology

Microsyster (Advice on using micro computers) – Wesley House, Wild Court (off Kingsway), London WC2 (01-430-0655)
Women's Computer Centre (same address as above)

Theatre

Women in Entertainment (National Pressure Group) – 7 Thorpe Close, London (01-969-2292)
Women Live in Scotland – 11a Forth St, Edinburgh 1 (031-637-9311)

Violence against women (see also 'Battered women' and 'Rape')

Incest Survivors Group Campaign and Self Help –
c/o A Woman's Place, Hungerford House, Victoria
Embankment, London WC2

Women's centres

England

Bradford – 75 Little Horton Lane, Bradford
(0274-736156)
Brighton – Basement, 6 Marlborough Place, Brighton,
Sussex (0273-600526)
Bristol – 44 The Grove, Bristol 1 (0272-22760)
Cambridge – 49a Burleigh St (entrance in Paradise
St), Cambridge (0223-313675)
Cleveland – St Mary's Centre, 42/50 Corporation Rd,
Middlesborough
Coventry – 1d Victoria St, Hillfields, Coventry
(0203-555531)
Croydon – 13 Woodside Green, South Norwood,
Croydon SE25 (01-656-2369)
Derby – The Guildhall, Derby (0334-372545)
Durham: Women in Durham – c/o Durham Community
Bookshop, 85a New Elvet, Durham (0385-61183)
Leeds Women's Centre Group – c/o Leeds TUCRIC,
first floor, Market Buildings, Vicar Lane,
Leeds LS2 7JP
Leeds University Women's Centre – Flat 14,
23 Cromer Terrace, Leeds 2, or c/o SU Leeds
University (0532-433209)
Leicester – 13 Welford Rd, Leicester (0533-556099)

London central

A Woman's Place – Hungerford House, Victoria
Embankment, London WC2 (01-836-6081)

London local

Cromer St (Kings Cross) – 90 Cromer St, London WC1
(01-278-0120)
Greenwich (Mobile centre and newsletter) – 14 Ebdon
Way, Ferrier Estate, Greenwich, London SE3
(01-856-3808)
Hackney – 27 Hackney Grove, London E8 3NR
(01-986-0840)
Haringey – 40 Turnpike Lane, London N8
(01-889-3912)
Kentish Town (Women's workshop) – 169 Malden Rd,
London NW5 (01-267-0688)
Lewisham and Deptford – 74 Deptford High St,
London SE8 (01-692-1851)
North Paddington – 115 Portnall Rd, London W9
(01-969-8897)
Southwark (Women's centre and bus) – 26 Peckham
High St, London SE15 (01-701-2564)
Tonbridge Street (Kings Cross) – 71 Tonbridge St,
London WC1 (01-837-7509)
Waltham Forest – 5 Pretoria Avenue, London E17
(01-520-5318)
West London (Drop-in/cafe) – Metrostore,
231 The Vale, Acton, London W3 (01-743-0326)
Manchester (newsletter only) – c/o 7 Norman Rd,
Rusholme, Manchester 14
Milton Keynes – c/o Veronica Clare, 62 Fulwoods,
Rainbow Drive, Leadenham, Milton Keynes
(0908-604324)
Norwich (Women's educational and resource centre)
– 50 Bethel St, Norwich
Oxford – 35/37 Cowley Rd, (over Uhuru cafe), Oxford
(0865-48249)
Plymouth – Peacock Lane, Palace St, Plymouth
(0752-261251)

Southampton – 1a Bevois Valley Rd, Portswood,
Southampton (0703-29714)
York – 11 Holgate Rd, York

Ireland

Belfast – 18 Donegall St, Belfast BT1 2GP
(0232-243363)
Cork – The Women's Space, Quay Co-op,
24 Sullivan's Quay, Cork (Cork 967660)
Derry – 7–9 Artillery St, Derry (0504-267672)
Dublin – 53 Dame St, Dublin 2 (Dublin 710088)

Scotland

Cumbernauld – c/o Liz McLaren, 81 Rose St,
Condorrat, Cumbernauld (023-6735138)
Edinburgh – 61a Broughton St, Edinburgh
(031-557-3179)
Glasgow – 48 Miller St, Glasgow (041-221-1177)
Inverness (Local contact) – c/o Gale Chrisman, Flat 4,
10 Culduthel Rd, Inverness (0463-236347)

Wales

Cardiff – 2 Coburn St, Cathays, Cardiff (0222-374051)
Swansea – 58 Alexandra Rd, Swansea (0792-467365)

Women with disabilities

Gemma (Lesbians with difficulties) – BM Box 5700,
London WC1N 3XX
Liberation Network of People with Disabilities –
c/o Townsend House, Green Lanes, Marshfield,
Chippenham, Wiltshire
Sisters Against Disablement – c/o Mayrav Dover,
241 Albion Rd, London N16 (01-241-2263)

Work

Low Pay Unit – 9 Poland St, London W1
(01-437-1780)
Women in Manual Trades – 52/54 Featherstone St,
London EC1 (01-251-9192)

Young women

Asian Girls Project – East End Mission,
583 Commercial Rd, London E1 (01-790-3366)
Brook Advisory Centres (advice on contraception and
pregnancy, particularly for young people) –
Head Office, 153a East St, London SE17
(01-708-1234/1390)
Camden Girls' Centre Project (runs several groups for
Asian girls) – 4 Caversham Rd, London NW5
(01-267 2808)
The Children's Legal Centre (legal advice, and
campaigns on young people's rights) –
20 Compton Terrace, London N1 (01-359-6251
weekdays 2–5pm)
Gay Young Movement (for young lesbians and gay
men wanting to campaign for gay liberation) –
BM GYM, London WC1N 3XX
Highfields Girls' Venture (feminists girls young
women's project) – 3 Mill Hill Lane, Highfields,
Leicester (0533-556796)
National Association of Youth Clubs (offers
information and help with groups, clubs, girls'
projects, video hire, printed materials etc) – NAYC
Girls Work, 30 Peacock Lane, Leicester LE1 5NY
(0533-29514)
NAYPIC – (National Association of Young People In
Care) (local groups) – Salem House, 28a Manor
Row, Bradford BD1 4QU (0274-728484)
Working with Girls Newsletter (pull out posters,
readers' meetings) – available from NAYC, above.